# BORDERS.
## CLASSICS

# WILLIAM SHAKESPEARE

## The Sonnets

### and Other Love Poems

**BORDERS.**
CLASSICS

Please direct sales or editorial inquiries to:
BordersTradeBookInventoryQuestions@bordersgroupinc.com

This edition is published by
Borders Classics, an imprint of Borders Group, Inc.,
by special arrangement with
Ann Arbor Media Group, LLC
2500 South State Street, Ann Arbor, MI 48104

Printed and bound in the United States of America
by Edwards Brothers, Inc.

Quality Paperback ISBN13: 978-1-58726-358-3
ISBN10: 1-58726-358-0

10   09   08   07   06       10 9 8 7 6 5 4 3 2

# CONTENTS

# SONNETS

TO.THE.ONLIE.BEGETTER.OF.
THESE.INSUING.SONNETS.
MR. W. H. ALL.HAPPINESSE.
AND.THAT.ETERNITIE.
PROMISED.BY.
OUR.EVER-LIVING.POET.
WISHETH.
THE.WELL-WISHING.
ADVENTURER.IN.
SETTING.
FORTH.

T. T.


## 1

From fairest creatures we desire increase,
That thereby beauty's rose might never die,
But as the riper should by time decrease,
His tender heir might bear his memory;
But thou, contracted to thine own bright eyes,
Feed'st thy light's flame with self-substantial fuel,
Making a famine where abundance lies,
Thyself thy foe, to thy sweet self too cruel.
Thou that art now the world's fresh ornament
And only herald to the gaudy spring
Within thine own bud buriest thy content,
And, tender churl, mak'st waste in niggarding.
    Pity the world, or else this glutton be:
    To eat the world's due, by the grave and thee.

## 2

When forty winters shall besiege thy brow
And dig deep trenches in thy beauty's field,
Thy youth's proud livery, so gazed on now,
Will be a tattered weed, of small worth held.
Then being asked where all thy beauty lies,
Where all the treasure of thy lusty days,
To say within thine own deep-sunken eyes
Were an all-eating shame and thriftless praise.
How much more praise deserved thy beauty's use
If thou couldst answer 'This fair child of mine
Shall sum my count, and make my old excuse,'
Proving his beauty by succession thine.
    This were to be new made when thou art old,
    And see thy blood warm when thou feel'st it cold.

## 3

Look in thy glass, and tell the face thou viewest
Now is the time that face should form another,
Whose fresh repair if now thou not renewest
Thou dost beguile the world, unbless some mother.
For where is she so fair whose uneared womb
Disdains the tillage of thy husbandry?
Or who is he so fond will be the tomb
Of his self-love to stop posterity?
Thou art thy mother's glass, and she in thee
Calls back the lovely April of her prime;
So thou through windows of thine age shalt see,
Despite of wrinkles, this thy golden time.
    But if thou live remembered not to be,
    Die single, and thine image dies with thee.

# 4

Unthrifty loveliness, why dost thou spend
Upon thyself thy beauty's legacy?
Nature's bequest gives nothing, but doth lend,
And being frank, she lends to those are free.
Then, beauteous niggard, why dost thou abuse
The bounteous largess given thee to give?
Profitless usurer, why dost thou use
So great a sum of sums yet canst not live?
For having traffic with thyself alone,
Thou of thyself thy sweet self dost deceive.
Then how when nature calls thee to be gone:
What acceptable audit canst thou leave?
    The unused beauty must be tombed with thee,
    Which usèd, lives th'executor to be.

# 5

Those hours that with gentle work did frame
The lovely gaze where every eye doth dwell
Will play the tyrants to the very same,
And that unfair which fairly doth excel;
For never-resting time leads summer on
To hideous winter, and confounds him there,
Sap checked with frost, and lusty leaves quite gone,
Beauty o'ersnowed, and bareness everywhere.
Then were not summer's distillation left
A liquid prisoner pent in walls of glass,
Beauty's effect with beauty were bereft,
Nor it nor no remembrance what it was.
    But flowers distilled, though they with winter meet,
    Lose but their show; their substance still lives sweet.

## 6

Then let not winter's ragged hand deface
In thee thy summer ere thou be distilled.
Make sweet some vial, treasure thou some place
With beauty's treasure ere it be self-killed.
That use is not forbidden usury
Which happies those that pay the willing loan:
That's for thyself to breed another thee,
Or ten times happier, be it ten for one;
Ten times thyself were happier than thou art,
If ten of thine ten times refigured thee.
Then what could death do if thou shouldst depart,
Leaving thee living in posterity?
    Be not self-willed, for thou art much too fair
    To be death's conquest and make worms thine heir.

## 7

Lo, in the orient when the gracious light
Lifts up his burning head, each under eye
Doth homage to his new-appearing sight,
Serving with looks his sacred majesty,
And having climbed the steep-up heavenly hill,
Resembling strong youth in his middle age,
Yet mortal looks adore his beauty still,
Attending on his golden pilgrimage.
But when from highmost pitch, with weary car,
Like feeble age he reeleth from the day,
The eyes, 'fore duteous, now converted are
From his low tract, and look another way.
    So thou, thyself outgoing in thy noon,
    Unlooked on diest unless thou get a son.

## 8

Music to hear, why hear'st thou music sadly?
Sweets with sweets war not, joy delights in joy.
Why lov'st thou that which thou receiv'st not gladly,
Or else receiv'st with pleasure thine annoy?
If the true concord of well-tuned sounds
By unions married do offend thine ear,
They do but sweetly chide thee, who confounds
In singleness the parts that thou shouldst bear.
Mark how one string, sweet husband to another,
Strikes each in each by mutual ordering,
Resembling sire and child and happy mother,
Who all in one one pleasing note do sing;
    Whose speechless song, being many, seeming one,
    Sings this to thee: 'Thou single wilt prove none.'

## 9

Is it for fear to wet a widow's eye
That thou consum'st thyself in single life?
Ah, if thou issueless shall hap to die,
The world will wail thee like a makeless wife.
The world will be thy widow, and still weep
That thou no form of thee hast left behind,
When every private widow well may keep
By children's eyes, her husband's shape in mind.
Look what an unthrift in the world doth spend
Shifts but his place, for still the world enjoys it;
But beauty's waste hath in the world an end,
And kept unused, the user so destroys it.
    No love toward others in that bosom sits
    That on himself such murd'rous shame commits.

## 10

For shame deny that thou bear'st love to any,
Who for thyself art so unprovident.
Grant, if thou wilt, thou art beloved of many,
But that thou none lov'st is most evident;
For thou art so possessed with murd'rous hate
That 'gainst thyself thou stick'st not to conspire,
Seeking that beauteous roof to ruinate
Which to repair should be thy chief desire.
O, change thy thought, that I may change my mind!
Shall hate be fairer lodged than gentle love?
Be as thy presence is, gracious and kind,
Or to thyself at least kind-hearted prove.
    Make thee another self for love of me,
    That beauty still may live in thine or thee.

## 11

As fast as thou shalt wane, so fast thou grow'st
In one of thine from that which thou departest.
And that fresh blood which youngly thou bestow'st
Thou mayst call thine when thou from youth convertest.
Herein lives wisdom, beauty, and increase;
Without this, folly, age, and cold decay.
If all were minded so, the times should cease,
And threescore year would make the world away.
Let those whom nature hath not made for store,
Harsh, featureless, and rude, barrenly perish.
Look whom she best endowed, she gave the more,
Which bounteous gift thou shouldst in bounty cherish.
    She carved thee for her seal, and meant thereby
    Thou shouldst print more, nor let that copy die.

## 12

When I do count the clock that tells the time,
And see the brave day sunk in hideous night;
When I behold the violet past prime,
And sable curls all silvered o'er with white;
When lofty trees I see barren of leaves,
Which erst from heat did canopy the herd,
And summer's green all girded up in sheaves
Borne on the bier with white and bristly beard:
Then of thy beauty do I question make
That thou among the wastes of time must go,
Since sweets and beauties do themselves forsake,
And die as fast as they see others grow;
    And nothing 'gainst time's scythe can make defence.
    Save breed, to brave him when he takes thee hence.

## 13

O that you were yourself! But, love, you are
No longer yours than you yourself here live.
Against this coming end you should prepare,
And your sweet semblance to some other give.
So should that beauty which you hold in lease
Find no determination; then you were
Yourself again after yourself's decease,
When your sweet issue your sweet form should bear.
Who lets so fair a house fall to decay,
Which husbandry in honour might uphold
Against the stormy gusts of winter's day,
And barren rage of death's eternal cold?
    O, none but unthrifts, dear my love, you know.
    You had a father; let your son say so.

14

Not from the stars do I my judgment pluck,
And yet methinks I have astronomy;
But not to tell of good or evil luck,
Of plagues, of dearths, or season's quality.
Nor can I fortune to brief minutes tell,
Pointing to each his thunder, rain, and wind,
Or say with princes if it shall go well
By oft predict that I in heaven find;
But from thine eyes my knowledge I derive,
And, constant stars, in them I read such art
As truth and beauty shall together thrive
If from thyself to store thou wouldst convert.
    Or else of thee this I prognosticate;
    Thy end is truth's and beauty's doom and date.


15

When I consider every thing that grows
Holds in perfection but a little moment,
That this huge stage presenteth naught but shows
Whereon the stars in secret influence comment;
When I perceive that men as plants increase,
Cheerèd and checked even by the selfsame sky;
Vaunt in their youthful sap, at height decrease,
And wear their brave state out of memory:
Then the conceit of this inconstant stay
Sets you most rich in youth before my sight,
Where wasteful time debateth with decay
To change your day of youth to sullied night;
    And all in war with time for love of you,
    As he takes from you, I engraft you new.

## 16

But wherefore do not you a mightier way
Make war upon this bloody tyrant, time,
And fortify yourself in your decay
With means more blessèd than my barren rhyme ?
Now stand you on the top of happy hours,
And many maiden gardens yet unset
With virtuous wish would bear your living flowers,
Much liker than your painted counterfeit.
So should the lines of life that life repair
Which this time's pencil or my pupil pen
Neither in inward worth nor outward fair
Can make you live yourself in eyes of men.
    To give away yourself keeps yourself still,
    And you must live drawn by your own sweet skill.

## 17

Who will believe my verse in time to come
If it were filled with your most high deserts?—
Though yet, heaven knows, it is but as a tomb
Which hides your life, and shows not half your parts.
If I could write the beauty of your eyes
And in fresh numbers number all your graces,
The age to come would say 'This poet lies;
Such heavenly touches ne'er touched earthly faces.'
So should my papers, yellowed with their age,
Be scorned, like old men of less truth than tongue,
And your true rights be termed a poet's rage
And stretchèd metre of an antique song.
    But were some child of yours alive that time,
    You should live twice: in it, and in my rhyme.

## 18

Shall I compare thee to a summer's day?
Thou art more lovely and more temperate.
Rough winds do shake the darling buds of May,
And summer's lease hath all too short a date.
Sometime too hot the eye of heaven shines,
And often is his gold complexion dimmed;
And every fair from fair sometime declines,
By chance or nature's changing course untrimmed;
But thy eternal summer shall not fade
Nor lose possession of that fair thou ow'st,
Nor shall death brag thou wander'st in his shade
When in eternal lines to time thou grow'st,
    So long as men can breathe or eyes can see,
    So long lives this, and this gives life to thee.

## 19

Devouring time, blunt thou the lion's paws,
And make the earth devour her own sweet brood;
Pluck the keen teeth from the fierce tiger's jaws,
And burn the long-lived phoenix in her blood.
Make glad and sorry seasons as thou fleet'st,
And do whate'er thou wilt, swift-footed time,
To the wide world and all her fading sweets.
But I forbid thee one most heinous crime:
O, carve not with thy hours my love's fair brow,
Nor draw no lines there with thine antique pen.
Him in thy course untainted do allow
For beauty's pattern to succeeding men.
    Yet do thy worst, old time; despite thy wrong
    My love shall in my verse ever live young.

## 20

A woman's face with nature's own hand painted
Hast thou, the master-mistress of my passion;
A woman's gentle heart, but not acquainted
With shifting change as is false woman's fashion;
An eye more bright than theirs, less false in rolling,
Gilding the object whereupon it gazeth;
A man in hue, all hues in his controlling,
Which steals men's eyes, and women's souls amazeth.
And for a woman wert thou first created,
Till nature as she wrought thee fell a-doting,
And by addition me of thee defeated
By adding one thing to my purpose nothing.
    But since she pricked thee out for women's pleasure,
    Mine be thy love and thy love's use their treasure.

## 21

So is it not with me as with that muse
Stirred by a painted beauty to his verse,
Who heaven itself for ornament doth use,
And every fair with his fair doth rehearse,
Making a couplement of proud compare
With sun and moon, with earth, and sea's rich gems,
With April's first-born flowers, and all things rare
That heaven's air in this huge rondure hems.
O let me, true in love, but truly write,
And then believe me my love is as fair
As any mother's child, though not so bright
As those gold candles fixed in heaven's air.
    Let them say more that like of hearsay well;
    I will not praise that purpose not to sell.

## 22

My glass shall not persuade me I am old
So long as youth and thou are of one date;
But when in thee time's furrows I behold,
Then look I death my days should expiate.
For all that beauty that doth cover thee
Is but the seemly raiment of my heart,
Which in thy breast doth live, as thine in me;
How can I then be elder than thou art?
O therefore, love, be of thyself so wary
As I, not for myself, but for thee will,
Bearing thy heart, which I will keep so chary
As tender nurse her babe from faring ill.
    Presume not on thy heart when mine is slain:
    Thou gav'st me thine not to give back again.


## 23

As an unperfect actor on the stage
Who with his fear is put besides his part,
Or some fierce thing replete with too much rage
Whose strength's abundance weakens his own heart,
So I, for fear of trust, forget to say
The perfect ceremony of love's rite,
And in mine own love's strength seem to decay,
O'er-charg'd with burden of mine own love's might.
O let my books be then the eloquence
And dumb presagers of my speaking breast,
Who plead for love, and look for recompense
More than that tongue that more hath more expressed.
    O learn to read what silent love hath writ;
    To hear with eyes belongs to love's fine wit.

## 24

Mine eye hath played the painter, and hath steeled
Thy beauty's form in table of my heart.
My body is the frame wherein 'tis held,
And perspective it is best painter's art;
For through the painter must you see his skill
To find where your true image pictured lies,
Which in my bosom's shop is hanging still,
That hath his windows glazèd with thine eyes.
Now see what good turns eyes for eyes have done:
Mine eyes have drawn thy shape, and thine for me
Are windows to my breast, wherethrough the sun
Delights to peep, to gaze therein on thee.
    Yet eyes this cunning want to grace their art:
    They draw but what they see, know not the heart.

## 25

Let those who are in favour with their stars
Of public honour and proud titles boast,
Whilst I, whom fortune of such triumph bars,
Unlooked-for joy in that I honour most.
Great princes' favourites their fair leaves spread
But as the marigold at the sun's eye
And in themselves their pride lies burièd,
For at a frown they in their glory die.
The painful warrior famousèd for might,
After a thousand victories once foiled
Is from the book of honour razèd quite,
And all the rest forgot for which he toiled.
    Then happy I, that love and am beloved
    Where I may not remove nor be removed.

## 26

Lord of my love, to whom in vassalage
Thy merit hath my duty strongly knit,
To thee I send this written embassage
To witness duty, not to show my wit;
Duty so great which wit so poor as mine
May make seem bare in wanting words to show it,
But that I hope some good conceit of thine
In thy soul's thought, all naked, will bestow it,
Till whatsoever star that guides my moving
Points on me graciously with fair aspect,
And puts apparel on my tattered loving
To show me worthy of thy sweet respect.
    Then may I dare to boast how I do love thee;
    Till then, not show my head where thou mayst prove me.

## 27

Weary with toil I haste me to my bed,
The dear repose for limbs with travel tired;
But then begins a journey in my head
To work my mind when body's work's expired;
For then my thoughts, from far where I abide,
Intend a zealous pilgrimage to thee,
And keep my drooping eyelids open wide,
Looking on darkness which the blind do see:
Save that my soul's imaginary sight
Presents thy shadow to my sightless view,
Which like a jewel hung in ghastly night
Makes black night beauteous and her old face new.
    Lo, thus by day my limbs, by night my mind,
    For thee, and for myself, no quiet find.

## 28

How can I then return in happy plight,
That am debarred the benefit of rest,
When day's oppression is not eased by night,
But day by night and night by day oppressed,
And each, though enemies to either's reign,
Do in consent shake hands to torture me,
The one by toil, the other to complain
How far I toil, still farther off from thee?
I tell the day to please him thou art bright,
And do'st him grace when clouds do blot the heaven;
So flatter I the swart-complexioned night
When sparkling stars twire not thou gild'st the even.
    But day doth daily draw my sorrows longer,
    And night doth nightly make grief's strength seem stronger.

## 29

When in disgrace with fortune and men's eyes,
I all alone beweep my outcast state,
And trouble deaf heaven with my bootless cries,
And look upon myself and curse my fate,
Wishing me like to one more rich in hope,
Featured like him, like him with friends possessed,
Desiring this man's art and that man's scope,
With what I most enjoy contented least:
Yet in these thoughts myself almost despising,
Haply I think on thee, and then my state,
Like to the lark at break of day arising
From sullen earth, sings hymns at heaven's gate;
    For thy sweet love remembered such wealth brings
    That then I scorn to change my state with kings'.

## 30

When to the sessions of sweet silent thought
I summon up remembrance of things past,
I sigh the lack of many a thing I sought,
And with old woes new wail my dear time's waste.
Then can I drown an eye unused to flow
For precious friends hid in death's dateless night,
And weep afresh love's long-since-cancelled woe,
And moan th' expense of many a vanished sight.
Then can I grieve at grievances foregone,
And heavily from woe to woe tell o'er
The sad account of fore-bemoanèd moan,
Which I new pay as if not paid before.
    But if the while I think on thee, dear friend,
    All losses are restored, and sorrows end.

## 31

Thy bosom is endearèd with all hearts
Which I by lacking have supposèd dead,
And there reigns love, and all love's loving parts,
And all those friends which I thought burièd.
How many a holy and obsequious tear
Hath dear religious love stol'n from mine eye
As interest of the dead, which now appear
But things removed that hidden in thee lie!
Thou art the grave where buried love doth live,
Hung with the trophies of my lovers gone,
Who all their parts of me to thee did give:
That due of many now is thine alone.
    Their images I loved I view in thee,
    And thou, all they, hast all the all of me.

## 32

If thou survive my well-contented day
When that churl death my bones with dust shall cover,
And shalt by fortune once more resurvey
These poor rude lines of thy deceased lover,
Compare them with the bett'ring of the time,
And though they be outstripped by every pen,
Reserve them for my love, not for their rhyme
Exceeded by the height of happier men.
O then vouchsafe me but this loving thought:
'Had my friend's muse grown with this growing age,
A dearer birth than this his love had brought
To march in ranks of better equipage;
    But since he died, and poets better prove,
    Theirs for their style I'll read, his for his love.'

## 33

Full many a glorious morning have I seen
Flatter the mountain tops with sovereign eye,
Kissing with golden face the meadows green,
Gilding pale streams with heavenly alchemy;
Anon permit the basest clouds to ride
With ugly rack on his celestial face,
And from the forlorn world his visage hide,
Stealing unseen to west with this disgrace.
Even so my sun one early morn did shine
With all triumphant splendour on my brow;
But out, alack, he was but one hour mine;
The region cloud hath masked him from me now.
    Yet him for this my love no whit disdaineth:
    Suns of the world may stain when heaven's sun staineth.

## 34

Why didst thou promise such a beauteous day
And make me travel forth without my cloak,
To let base clouds o'ertake me in my way,
Hiding thy brav'ry in their rotten smoke?
'Tis not enough that through the cloud thou break
To dry the rain on my storm-beaten face,
For no man well of such a salve can speak
That heals the wound and cures not the disgrace.
Nor can thy shame give physic to my grief;
Though thou repent, yet I have still the loss.
Th'offender's sorrow lends but weak relief
To him that bears the strong offence's cross.
    Ah, but those tears are pearl which thy love sheds,
    And they are rich, and ransom all ill deeds.

## 35

No more be grieved at that which thou hast done:
Roses have thorns, and silver fountains mud.
Clouds and eclipses stain both moon and sun,
And loathsome canker lives in sweetest bud.
All men make faults, and even I in this,
Authorising thy trespass with compare,
Myself corrupting salving thy amiss,
Excusing thy sins more than thy sins are;
For to thy sensual fault I bring in sense—
Thy adverse party is thy advocate—
And 'gainst myself a lawful plea commence.
Such civil war is in my love and hate
    That I an accessory needs must be
    To that sweet thief which sourly robs from me.

## 36

Let me confess that we two must be twain
Although our undivided loves are one;
So shall those blots that do with me remain
Without thy help by me be borne alone.
In our two loves there is but one respect,
Though in our lives a separable spite
Which, though it alter not love's sole effect,
Yet doth it steal sweet hours from love's delight.
I may not evermore acknowledge thee
Lest my bewailed guilt should do thee shame,
Nor thou with public kindness honour me
Unless thou take that honour from thy name.
　　But do not so. I love thee in such sort
　　As, thou being mine, mine is thy good report.

## 37

As a decrepit father takes delight
To see his active child do deeds of youth,
So I, made lame by fortune's dearest spite,
Take all my comfort of thy worth and truth;
For whether beauty, birth, or wealth, or wit,
Or any of these all, or all, or more,
Entitled in thy parts do crownèd sit,
I make my love engrafted to this store.
So then I am not lame, poor, nor despised,
Whilst that this shadow doth such substance give
That I in thy abundance am sufficed
And by a part of all thy glory live.
　　Look what is best, that best I wish in thee;
　　This wish I have, then ten times happy me.

## 38

How can my muse want subject to invent
While thou dost breathe, that pour'st into my verse
Thine own sweet argument, too excellent
For every vulgar paper to rehearse?
O, give thyself the thanks if aught in me
Worthy perusal stand against thy sight;
For who's so dumb that cannot write to thee,
When thou thyself dost give invention light?
Be thou the tenth muse, ten times more in worth
Than those old nine which rhymers invocate,
And he that calls on thee, let him bring forth
Eternal numbers to outlive long date.
　　If my slight muse do please these curious days,
　　The pain be mine, but thine shall be the praise.

## 39

O, how thy worth with manners may I sing
When thou art all the better part of me?
What can mine own praise to mine own self bring,
And what is't but mine own when I praise thee?
Even for this let us divided live,
And our dear love lose name of single one,
That by this separation I may give
That due to thee which thou deserv'st alone.
O absence, what a torment wouldst thou prove
Were it not thy sour leisure gave sweet leave
To entertain the time with thoughts of love,
Which time and thoughts so sweetly doth deceive,
　　And that thou teachest how to make one twain
　　By praising him here who doth hence remain!

## 40

Take all my loves, my love, yea, take them all:
What hast thou then more than thou hadst before?
No love, my love, that thou mayst true love call—
All mine was thine before thou hadst this more.
Then if for my love thou my love receivest,
I cannot blame thee for my love thou usest;
But yet be blamed if thou this self deceivest
By wilful taste of what thyself refusest.
I do forgive thy robb'ry, gentle thief,
Although thou steal thee all my poverty;
And yet love knows it is a greater grief          .
To bear love's wrong than hate's known injury.
    Lascivious grace, in whom all ill well shows,
    Kill me with spites, yet we must not be foes.

## 41

Those pretty wrongs that liberty commits
When I am sometime absent from thy heart
Thy beauty and thy years full well befits,
For still temptation follows where thou art.
Gentle thou art, and therefore to be won;
Beauteous thou art, therefore to be assailed;
And when a woman woos, what woman's son
Will sourly leave her till he have prevailed?
Ah me, but yet thou mightst my seat forbear,
And chide thy beauty and thy straying youth
Who lead thee in their riot even there
Where thou art forced to break a two-fold troth:
    Hers, by thy beauty tempting her to thee,
    Thine, by thy beauty being false to me.

## 42

That thou hast her, it is not all my grief,
And yet it may be said I loved her dearly;
That she hath thee is of my wailing chief,
A loss in love that touches me more nearly.
Loving offenders, thus I will excuse ye:
Thou dost love her because thou know'st I love her,
And for my sake even so doth she abuse me,
Suff'ring my friend for my sake to approve her.
If I lose thee, my loss is my love's gain,
And losing her, my friend hath found that loss:
Both find each other, and I lose both twain,
And both for my sake lay on me this cross.
    But here's the joy: my friend and I are one.
    Sweet flattery! Then she loves but me alone.

## 43

When most I wink, then do mine eyes best see,
For all the day they view things unrespected;
But when I sleep, in dreams they look on thee,
And, darkly bright, are bright in dark directed.
Then thou, whose shadow shadows doth make bright,
How would thy shadow's form form happy show
To the clear day with thy much clearer light,
When to unseeing eyes thy shade shines so!
How would, I say, mine eyes be blessed made
By looking on thee in the living day,
When in dead night thy fair imperfect shade
Through heavy sleep on sightless eyes doth stay!
    All days are nights to see, till I see thee,
    And nights bright days when dreams do show thee me.

## 44

If the dull substance of my flesh were thought,
Injurious distance should not stop my way;
For then, despite of space, I would be brought
From limits far remote where thou dost stay.
No matter then although my foot did stand
Upon the farthest earth removed from thee;
For nimble thought can jump both sea and land
As soon as think the place where he would be.
But ah, thought kills me that I am not thought,
To leap large lengths of miles when thou art gone,
But that, so much of earth and water wrought,
I must attend time's leisure with my moan,
    Receiving naught by elements so slow
    But heavy tears, badges of either's woe.

## 45

The other two, slight air and purging fire,
Are both with thee wherever I abide;
The first my thought, the other my desire,
These present-absent with swift motion slide;
For when these quicker elements are gone
In tender embassy of love to thee,
My life, being made of four, with two alone
Sinks down to death, oppressed with melancholy,
Until life's composition be recured
By those swift messengers returned from thee,
Who even but now come back again assured
Of thy fair health, recounting it to me.
    This told, I joy; but then no longer glad,
    I send them back again and straight grow sad.

## 46

Mine eye and heart are at a mortal war
How to divide the conquest of thy sight.
Mine eye my heart thy picture's sight would bar,
My heart, mine eye the freedom of that right.
My heart doth plead that thou in him dost lie,
A closet never pierced with crystal eyes;
But the defendant doth that plea deny,
And says in him thy fair appearance lies.
To 'cide this title is impannellèd
A quest of thoughts, all tenants to the heart,
And by their verdict is determinèd
The clear eye's moiety and the dear heart's part,
    As thus: mine eye's due is thy outward part,
    And my heart's right thy inward love of heart.

## 47

Betwixt mine eye and heart a league is took,
And each doth good turns now unto the other.
When that mine eye is famished for a look,
Or heart in love with sighs himself doth smother,
With my love's picture then my eye doth feast,
And to the painted banquet bids my heart.
Another time mine eye is my heart's guest
And in his thoughts of love doth share a part.
So either by thy picture or my love,
Thyself away art present still with me;
For thou not farther than my thoughts canst move,
And I am still with them, and they with thee;
    Or if they sleep, thy picture in my sight
    Awakes my heart to heart's and eye's delight.

## 48

How careful was I when I took my way
Each trifle under truest bars to thrust,
That to my use it might unused stay
From hands of falsehood, in sure wards of trust.
But thou, to whom my jewels trifles are,
Most worthy comfort, now my greatest grief,
Thou best of dearest and mine only care
Art left the prey of every vulgar thief.
Thee have I not locked up in any chest
Save where thou art not, though I feel thou art—
Within the gentle closure of my breast,
From whence at pleasure thou mayst come and part;
 And even thence thou wilt be stol'n, I fear,
 For truth proves thievish for a prize so dear.

## 49

Against that time—if ever that time come—
When I shall see thee frown on my defects,
Whenas thy love hath cast his utmost sum,
Called to that audit by advised respects;
Against that time when thou shalt strangely pass
And scarcely greet me with that sun, thine eye,
When love converted from the thing it was
Shall reasons find of settled gravity:
Against that time do I ensconce me here
Within the knowledge of mine own desert,
And this my hand against myself uprear
To guard the lawful reasons on thy part.
 To leave poor me thou hast the strength of laws,
 Since why to love I can allege no cause.

## 50

How heavy do I journey on the way,
When what I seek—my weary travel's end—
Doth teach that ease and that repose to say
'Thus far the miles are measured from thy friend.'
The beast that bears me, tired with my woe,
Plods dully on to bear that weight in me,
As if by some instinct the wretch did know
His rider loved not speed, being made from thee.
The bloody spur cannot provoke him on
That sometimes anger thrusts into his hide,
Which heavily he answers with a groan
More sharp to me than spurring to his side;
    For that same groan doth put this in my mind:
    My grief lies onward and my joy behind.

## 51

Thus can my love excuse the slow offence
Of my dull bearer when from thee I speed:
From where thou art why should I haste me thence?
Till I return, of posting is no need.
O what excuse will my poor beast then find
When swift extremity can seem but slow?
Then should I spur, though mounted on the wind;
In wingèd speed no motion shall I know.
Then can no horse with my desire keep pace;
Therefore desire, of perfect'st love being made,
Shall neigh no dull flesh in his fiery race;
But love, for love, thus shall excuse my jade:
    Since from thee going he went wilful-slow,
    Towards thee I'll run and give him leave to go.

## 52

So am I as the rich whose blessed key
Can bring him to his sweet up-lockèd treasure,
The which he will not ev'ry hour survey,
For blunting the fine point of seldom pleasure.
Therefore are feasts so solemn and so rare
Since, seldom coming, in the long year set
Like stones of worth they thinly placèd are,
Or captain jewels in the carcanet.
So is the time that keeps you as my chest,
Or as the wardrobe which the robe doth hide,
To make some special instant special blest,
By new unfolding his imprisoned pride.
　　　Blessèd are you whose worthiness gives scope,
　　　Being had, to triumph; being lacked, to hope.

## 53

What is your substance, whereof are you made,
That millions of strange shadows on you tend?
Since every one hath, every one, one's shade,
And you, but one, can every shadow lend.
Describe Adonis, and the counterfeit
Is poorly imitated after you.
On Helen's cheek all art of beauty set,
And you in Grecian tires are painted new.
Speak of the spring and foison of the year:
The one doth shadow of your beauty show,
The other as your bounty doth appear;
And you in every blessèd shape we know.
　　　In all external grace you have some part,
　　　But you like none, none you, for constant heart.

## 54

O how much more doth beauty beauteous seem
By that sweet ornament which truth doth give!
The rose looks fair, but fairer we it deem
For that sweet odour which doth in it live.
The canker blooms have full as deep a dye
As the perfumèd tincture of the roses,
Hang on such thorns, and play as wantonly
When summer's breath their maskèd buds discloses;
But for their virtue only is their show
They live unwooed and unrespected fade,
Die to themselves. Sweet roses do not so;
Of their sweet deaths are sweetest odours made:
    And so of you, beauteous and lovely youth,
    When that shall fade, by verse distils your truth.

## 55

Not marble nor the gilded monuments
Of princes shall outlive this powerful rhyme,
But you shall shine more bright in these contents
Than unswept stone besmeared with sluttish time.
When wasteful war shall statues overturn,
And broils root out the work of masonry,
Nor Mars his sword nor war's quick fire shall burn
The living record of your memory.
'Gainst death and all oblivious enmity
Shall you pace forth; your praise shall still find room
Even in the eyes of all posterity
That wear this world out to the ending doom.
    So, till the judgment that yourself arise,
    You live in this, and dwell in lovers' eyes.

## 56

Sweet love, renew thy force. Be it not said
Thy edge should blunter be than appetite,
Which but today by feeding is allayed,
Tomorrow sharpened in his former might.
So, love, be thou; although today them fill
Thy hungry eyes even till they wink with fulness,
Tomorrow see again, and do not kill
The spirit of love with a perpetual dulness.
Let this sad int'rim like the ocean be
Which parts the shore where two contracted new
Come daily to the banks, that when they see
Return of love, more blessed may be the view;
    Or call it winter, which, being full of care,
    Makes summer's welcome, thrice more wished, more rare.

## 57

Being your slave, what should I do but tend
Upon the hours and times of your desire?
I have no precious time at all to spend,
Nor services to do, till you require;
Nor dare I chide the world-without-end hour
Whilst I, my sovereign, watch the clock for you,
Nor think the bitterness of absence sour
When you have bid your servant once adieu.
Nor dare I question with my jealous thought
Where you may be, or your affairs suppose,
But like a sad slave stay and think of naught
Save, where you are, how happy you make those.
    So true a fool is love that in your will,
    Though you do anything, he thinks no ill.

## 58

That god forbid, that made me first your slave,
I should in thought control your times of pleasure,
Or at your hand th'account of hours to crave,
Being your vassal bound to stay your leisure.
O let me suffer, being at your beck,
Th'imprisoned absence of your liberty,
And patience, tame to sufferance, bide each check,
Without accusing you of injury.
Be where you list, your charter is so strong
That you yourself may privilege your time
To what you will; to you it doth belong
Yourself to pardon of self-doing crime.
    I am to wait, though waiting so be hell,
    Not blame your pleasure, be it ill or well.

## 59

If there be nothing new, but that which is
Hath been before, how are our brains beguiled,
Which, labouring for invention, bear amiss
The second burthen of a former child!
O that record could with a backward look
Even of five hundred courses of the sun
Show me your image in some antique book
Since mind at first in character was done,
That I might see what the old world could say
To this composèd wonder of your frame;
Whether we are mended or whe'er better they,
Or whether revolution be the same.
    O, sure I am the wits of former days
    To subjects worse have given admiring praise.

## 60

Like as the waves make towards the pebbled shore,
So do our minutes hasten to their end,
Each changing place with that which goes before;
In sequent toil all forwards do contend.
Nativity, once in the main of light,
Crawls to maturity, wherewith being crowned
Crookèd eclipses 'gainst his glory fight,
And time that gave doth now his gift confound.
Time doth transfix the flourish set on youth,
And delves the parallels in beauty's brow;
Feeds on the rarities of nature's truth,
And nothing stands but for his scythe to mow.
    And yet to times in hope my verse shall stand,
    Praising thy worth despite his cruel hand.

## 61

Is it thy will thy image should keep open
My heavy eyelids to the weary night?
Dost thou desire my slumbers should be broken
While shadows like to thee do mock my sight?
Is it thy spirit that thou send'st from thee
So far from home into my deeds to pry,
To find out shames and idle hours in me,
The scope and tenor of thy jealousy?
O no; thy love, though much, is not so great.
It is my love that keeps mine eye awake,
Mine own true love that doth my rest defeat,
To play the watchman ever for thy sake.
    For thee watch I whilst thou dost wake elsewhere,
    From me far off, with others all too near.

## 62

Sin of self-love possesseth all mine eye,
And all my soul, and all my every part;
And for this sin there is no remedy,
It is so grounded inward in my heart.
Methinks no face so gracious is as mine,
No shape so true, no truth of such account,
And for myself mine own worth to define
As I all other in all worths surmount.
But when my glass shows me myself indeed,
Beated and chapped with tanned antiquity,
Mine own self-love quite contrary I read;
Self so self-loving were iniquity.
 'Tis thee, myself, that for myself I praise,
 Painting my age with beauty of thy days.

## 63

Against my love shall be as I am now,
With time's injurious hand crushed and o'erworn;
When hours have drained his blood and filled his brow
With lines and wrinkles; when his youthful morn
Hath travelled on to age's steepy night,
And all those beauties whereof now he's king
Are vanishing, or vanished out of sight,
Stealing away the treasure of his spring:
For such a time do I now fortify
Against confounding age's cruel knife,
That he shall never cut from memory
My sweet love's beauty, though my lover's life.
 His beauty shall in these black lines be seen,
 And they shall live, and he in them still green.

## 64

When I have seen by time's fell hand defaced
The rich proud cost of outworn buried age;
When sometime-lofty towers I see down razed,
And brass eternal slave to mortal rage;
When I have seen the hungry ocean gain
Advantage on the kingdom of the shore,
And the firm soil win of the wat'ry main,
Increasing store with loss and loss with store;
When I have seen such interchange of state,
Or state itself confounded to decay,
Ruin hath taught me thus to ruminate:
That time will come and take my love away.
    This thought is as a death, which cannot choose
    But weep to have that which it fears to lose.

## 65

Since brass, nor stone, nor earth, nor boundless sea,
But sad mortality o'ersways their power,
How with this rage shall beauty hold a plea,
Whose action is no stronger than a flower?
O how shall summer's honey breath hold out
Against the wrackful siege of battering days
When rocks impregnable are not so stout,
Nor gates of steel so strong, but time decays?
O fearful meditation! Where, alack,
Shall time's best jewel from time's chest lie hid,
Or what strong hand can hold his swift foot back,
Or who his spoil of beauty can forbid?
    O none, unless this miracle have might:
    That in black ink my love may still shine bright.

## 66

Tired with all these, for restful death I cry:
As, to behold desert a beggar born,
And needy nothing trimmed in jollity,
And purest faith unhappily forsworn,
And gilded honour shamefully misplaced,
And maiden virtue rudely strumpeted,
And right perfection wrongfully disgraced,
And strength by limping sway disablèd,
And art made tongue-tied by authority,
And folly, doctor-like, controlling skill,
And simple truth miscalled simplicity,
And captive good attending captain ill.
 Tired with all these, from these would I be gone,
 Save that to die I leave my love alone.

## 67

Ah, wherefore with infection should he live
And with his presence grace impiety,
That sin by him advantage should achieve
And lace itself with his society?
Why should false painting imitate his cheek,
And steal dead seeming of his living hue?
Why should poor beauty indirectly seek
Roses of shadow, since his rose is true?
Why should he live now nature bankrupt is,
Beggared of blood to blush through lively veins,
For she hath no exchequer now but his,
And proud of many, lives upon his gains?
 O, him she stores to show what wealth she had
 In days long since, before these last so bad.

## 68

Thus is his cheek the map of days outworn,
When beauty lived and died as flowers do now,
Before these bastard signs of fair were borne
Or durst inhabit on a living brow;
Before the golden tresses of the dead,
The right of sepulchres, were shorn away
To live a second life on second head;
Ere beauty's dead fleece made another gay.
In him those holy antique hours are seen
Without all ornament, itself and true,
Making no summer of another's green,
Robbing no old to dress his beauty new;
    And him as for a map doth nature store,
    To show false art what beauty was of yore.

## 69

Those parts of thee that the world's eye doth view
Want nothing that the thought of hearts can mend.
All tongues, the voice of souls, give thee that due,
Utt'ring bare truth even so as foes commend.
Thy outward thus with outward praise is crowned,
But those same tongues that give thee so thine own,
In other accents do this praise confound
By seeing farther than the eye hath shown.
They look into the beauty of thy mind,
And that in guess they measure by thy deeds.
Then, churls, their thoughts—although their eyes were kind—
To thy fair flower add the rank smell of weeds.
    But why thy odour matcheth not thy show,
    The soil is this: that thou dost common grow.

## 70

That thou art blamed shall not be thy defect,
For slander's mark was ever yet the fair.
The ornament of beauty is suspect,
A crow that flies in heaven's sweetest air.
So thou be good, slander doth but approve
Thy worth the greater, being wooed of time;
For canker vice the sweetest buds doth love,
And thou present'st a pure unstainèd prime.
Thou hast passed by the ambush of young days
Either not assailed, or victor being charged;
Yet this thy praise cannot be so thy praise
To tie up envy, evermore enlarged.
    If some suspect of ill masked not thy show,
    Then thou alone kingdoms of hearts shouldst owe.

## 71

No longer mourn for me when I am dead
Than you shall hear the surly sullen bell
Give warning to the world that I am fled
From this vile world with vilest worms to dwell.
Nay, if you read this line, remember not
The hand that writ it; for I love you so
That I in your sweet thoughts would be forgot
If thinking on me then should make you woe.
O, if, I say, you look upon this verse
When I perhaps compounded am with clay,
Do not so much as my poor name rehearse,
But let your love even with my life decay,
    Lest the wise world should look into your moan
    And mock you with me after I am gone.

## 72

O, lest the world should task you to recite
What merit lived in me that you should love,
After my death, dear love, forget me quite;
For you in me can nothing worthy prove—
Unless you would devise some virtuous lie
To do more for me than mine own desert,
And hang more praise upon deceasèd I
Than niggard truth would willingly impart.
O, lest your true love may seem false in this,
That you for love speak well of me untrue,
My name be buried where my body is,
And live no more to shame nor me nor you;
    For I am shamed by that which I bring forth,
    And so should you, to love things nothing worth.

## 73

That time of year thou mayst in me behold
When yellow leaves, or none, or few, do hang
Upon those boughs which shake against the cold,
Bare ruined choirs where late the sweet birds sang.
In me thou seest the twilight of such day
As after sunset fadeth in the west,
Which by and by black night doth take away,
Death's second self, that seals up all in rest.
In me thou seest the glowing of such fire
That on the ashes of his youth doth lie
As the death-bed whereon it must expire,
Consumed with that which it was nourished by.
    This thou perceiv'st which makes thy love more strong,
    To love that well which thou must leave ere long.

## 74

But be contented when that fell arrest
Without all bail shall carry me away.
My life hath in this line some interest,
Which for memorial still with thee shall stay.
When thou reviewest this, thou dost review
The very part was consecrate to thee.
The earth can have but earth, which is his due;
My spirit is thine, the better part of me.
So then thou hast but lost the dregs of life,
The prey of worms, my body being dead,
The coward conquest of a wretch's knife,
Too base of thee to be rememberèd.
    The worth of that is that which it contains,
    And that is this, and this with thee remains.

## 75

So are you to my thoughts as food to life,
Or as sweet-seasoned showers are to the ground;
And for the peace of you I hold such strife
As 'twixt a miser and his wealth is found:
Now proud as an enjoyer, and anon
Doubting the filching age will steal his treasure;
Now counting best to be with you alone,
Then bettered that the world may see my pleasure;
Sometime all full with feasting on your sight,
And by and by clean starvèd for a look;
Possessing or pursuing no delight
Save what is had or must from you be took.
    Thus do I pine and surfeit day by day,
    Or gluttoning on all, or all away.

## 76

Why is my verse so barren of new pride,
So far from variation or quick change?
Why, with the time, do I not glance aside
To new-found methods and to compounds strange?
Why write I still all one, ever the same,
And keep invention in a noted weed,
That every word doth almost tell my name,
Showing their birth and where they did proceed?
O know, sweet love, I always write of you,
And you and love are still my argument;
So all my best is dressing old words new,
Spending again what is already spent;
    For as the sun is daily new and old,
    So is my love, still telling what is told.

## 77

Thy glass will show thee how thy beauties wear,
Thy dial how thy precious minutes waste,
The vacant leaves thy mind's imprint will bear,
And of this book this learning mayst thou taste:
The wrinkles which thy glass will truly show
Of mouthèd graves will give thee memory;
Thou by thy dial's shady stealth mayst know
Time's thievish progress to eternity.
Look what thy memory cannot contain
Commit to these waste blanks, and thou shalt find
Those children nursed, delivered from thy brain,
To take a new acquaintance of thy mind.
    These offices so oft as thou wilt look
    Shall profit thee and much enrich thy book.

## 78

So oft have I invoked thee for my muse
And found such fair assistance in my verse
As every alien pen hath got my use,
And under thee their poesy disperse.
Thine eyes, that taught the dumb on high to sing
And heavy ignorance aloft to fly,
Have added feathers to the learned's wing
And given grace a double majesty.
Yet be most proud of that which I compile,
Whose influence is thine and born of thee.
In others' works thou dost but mend the style,
And arts with thy sweet graces gracèd be;
  But thou art all my art, and dost advance
  As high as learning my rude ignorance.

## 79

Whilst I alone did call upon thy aid
My verse alone had all thy gentle grace;
But now my gracious numbers are decayed,
And my sick muse doth give another place.
I grant, sweet love, thy lovely argument
Deserves the travail of a worthier pen,
Yet what of thee thy poet doth invent
He robs thee of, and pays it thee again.
He lends thee virtue, and he stole that word
From thy behaviour; beauty doth he give,
And found it in thy cheek: he can afford
No praise to thee but what in thee doth live.
  Then thank him not for that which he doth say,
  Since what he owes thee thou thyself dost pay.

## 80

O, how faint when I of you do write,
Knowing a better spirit doth use your name,
And in the praise thereof spends all his might,
To make me tongue-tied, speaking of your fame!
But since your worth (wide as the ocean is)
The humble as the proudest sail doth bear,
My saucy barque, inferior far to his,
On your broad main doth wilfully appear.
Your shallowest help will hold me up afloat
Whilst he upon your soundless deep doth ride;
Or, being wrecked, I am a worthless boat,
He of tall building and of goodly pride.
 Then if he thrive, and I be cast away,
 The worst was this: my love was my decay.

## 81

Or I shall live your epitaph to make,
Or you survive when I in earth am rotten.
From hence your memory death cannot take,
Although in me each part will be forgotten.
Your name from hence immortal life shall have,
Though I, once gone, to all the world must die.
The earth can yield me but a common grave
When you entombèd in men's eyes shall lie.
Your monument shall be my gentle verse,
Which eyes not yet created shall o'er-read,
And tongues to be your being shall rehearse
When all the breathers of this world are dead.
 You still shall live—such virtue hath my pen—
 Where breath most breathes, even in the mouths of men.

## 82

I grant thou wert not married to my muse,
And therefore mayst without attaint o'erlook
The dedicated words which writers use
Of their fair subject, blessing every book.
Thou art as fair in knowledge as in hue,
Finding thy worth a limit past my praise,
And therefore art enforced to seek anew
Some fresher stamp of these time-bettering days.
And do so, love; yet when they have devised
What strainèd touches rhetoric can lend,
Thou, truly fair, wert truly sympathized
In true plain words by thy true-telling friend;
      And their gross painting might be better used
      Where cheeks need blood: in thee it is abused.

## 83

I never saw that you did painting need,
And therefore to your fair no painting set.
I found—or thought I found—you did exceed
The barren tender of a poet's debt;
And therefore have I slept in your report:
That you yourself, being extant, well might show
How far a modern quill doth come too short,
Speaking of worth, what worth in you doth grow.
This silence for my sin you did impute,
Which shall be most my glory, being dumb;
For I impair not beauty, being mute,
When others would give life, and bring a tomb.
      There lives more life in one of your fair eyes
      Than both your poets can in praise devise.

## 84

Who is it that says most which can say more
Than this rich praise: that you alone are you,
In whose confine immurèd is the store
Which should example where your equal grew?
Lean penury within that pen doth dwell
That to his subject lends not some small glory;
But he that writes of you, if he can tell
That you are you, so dignifies his story.
Let him but copy what in you is writ,
Not making worse what nature made so clear,
And such a counterpart shall fame his wit,
Making his style admirèd everywhere.
    You to your beauteous blessings add a curse,
    Being fond on praise, which makes your praises worse.

## 85

My tongue-tied muse in manners holds her still
While comments of your praise, richly compiled,
Reserve their character with golden quill
And precious phrase by all the muses filed.
I think good thoughts whilst other write good words,
And like unlettered clerk still cry 'Amen'
To every hymn that able spirit affords
In polished form of well-refinèd pen.
Hearing you praised I say ' 'Tis so, 'tis true,'
And to the most of praise add something more;
But that is in my thought, whose love to you,
Though words come hindmost, holds his rank before.
    Then others for the breath of words respect,
    Me for my dumb thoughts, speaking in effect.

## 86

Was it the proud full sail of his great verse
Bound for the prize of all-too-precious you
That did my ripe thoughts in my brain inhearse,
Making their tomb the womb wherein they grew?
Was it his spirit, by spirits taught to write
Above a mortal pitch, that struck me dead?
No, neither he nor his compeers by night
Giving him aid my verse astonishèd.
He nor that affable familiar ghost
Which nightly gulls him with intelligence,
As victors, of my silence cannnot boast;
I was not sick of any fear from thence.
    But when your countenance filed up his line,
    Then lacked I matter; that enfeebled mine.

## 87

Farewell—thou art too dear for my possessing,
And like enough thou know'st thy estimate.
The charter of thy worth gives thee releasing;
My bonds in thee are all determinate.
For how do I hold thee but by thy granting,
And for that riches where is my deserving?
The cause of this fair gift in me is wanting,
And so my patent back again is swerving.
Thyself thou gav'st, thy own worth then not knowing,
Or me to whom thou gav'st it else mistaking;
So thy great gift, upon misprision growing,
Comes home again, on better judgment making.
    Thus have I had thee as a dream doth flatter:
    In sleep a king, but waking no such matter.

## 88

When thou shalt be disposed to set me light
And place my merit in the eye of scorn,
Upon thy side against myself I'll fight,
And prove thee virtuous though thou art forsworn.
With mine own weakness being best acquainted,
Upon thy part I can set down a story
Of faults concealed wherein I am attainted,
That thou in losing me shall win much glory;
And I by this will be a gainer too;
For bending all my loving thoughts on thee,
The injuries that to myself I do,
Doing thee vantage, double vantage me.
    Such is my love, to thee I so belong,
    That for thy right myself will bear all wrong.

## 89

Say that thou didst forsake me for some fault,
And I will comment upon that offence;
Speak of my lameness, and I straight will halt,
Against thy reasons making no defence.
Thou canst not, love, disgrace me half so ill,
To set a form upon desirèd change,
As I'll myself disgrace, knowing thy will.
I will acquaintance strangle and look strange,
Be absent from thy walks, and in my tongue
Thy sweet belovèd name no more shall dwell,
Lest I, too much profane, should do it wrong,
And haply of our old acquaintance tell.
    For thee, against myself I'll vow debate;
    For I must ne'er love him whom thou dost hate.

## 90

Then hate me when thou wilt, if ever, now,
Now while the world is bent my deeds to cross,
Join with the spite of fortune, make me bow,
And do not drop in for an after-loss.
Ah do not, when my heart hath scaped this sorrow,
Come in the rearward of a conquered woe;
Give not a windy night a rainy morrow
To linger out a purposed overthrow.
If thou wilt leave me, do not leave me last,
When other petty griefs have done their spite,
But in the onset come; so shall I taste
At first the very worst of fortune's might,
       And other strains of woe, which now seem woe,
       Compared with loss of thee will not seem so.

## 91

Some glory in their birth, some in their skill,
Some in their wealth, some in their body's force,
Some in their garments (though new-fangled ill),
Some in their hawks and hounds, some in their horse,
And every humour hath his adjunct pleasure
Wherein it finds a joy above the rest.
But these particulars are not my measure;
All these I better in one general best.
Thy love is better than high birth to me,
Richer than wealth, prouder than garments' cost,
Of more delight than hawks and horses be,
And having thee of all men's pride I boast,
       Wretched in this alone: that thou mayst take
       All this away, and me most wretched make.

## 92

But do thy worst to steal thyself away,
For term of life thou art assurèd mine,
And life no longer than thy love will stay,
For it depends upon that love of thine.
Then need I not to fear the worst of wrongs
When in the least of them my life hath end.
I see a better state to me belongs
Than that which on thy humour doth depend.
Thou canst not vex me with inconstant mind,
Since that my life on thy revolt doth lie.
O, what a happy title do I find—
Happy to have thy love, happy to die!
 But what's so blessèd fair that fears no blot?
 Thou mayst be false, and yet I know it not.

## 93

So shall I live supposing thou art true
Like a deceivèd husband; so love's face
May still seem love to me, though altered new—
Thy looks with me, thy heart in other place.
For there can live no hatred in thine eye,
Therefore in that I cannot know thy change.
In many's looks the false heart's history
Is wri, in moods and frowns and wrinkles strange,
But heaven in thy creation did decree
That in thy face sweet love should ever dwell;
Whate'er thy thoughts or thy heart's workings be,
Thy looks should nothing thence but sweetness tell.
 How like Eve's apple doth thy beauty grow
 If thy sweet virtue answer not thy show!

## 94

They that have power to hurt and will do none,
That do not do the thing they most do show,
Who moving others are themselves as stone,
Unmoved, cold, and to temptation slow—
They rightly do inherit heaven's graces,
And husband nature's riches from expense;
They are the lords and owners of their faces,
Others but stewards of their excellence.
The summer's flower is to the summer sweet
Though to itself it only live and die,
But if that flower with base infection meet
The basest weed outbraves his dignity;
    For sweetest things turn sourest by their deeds:
    Lilies that fester smell far worse than weeds.

## 95

How sweet and lovely dost thou make the shame
Which, like a canker in the fragrant rose,
Doth spot the beauty of thy budding name!
O, in what sweets dost thou thy sins enclose!
That tongue that tells the story of thy days,
Making lascivious comments on thy sport,
Cannot dispraise, but in a kind of praise,
Naming thy name, blesses an ill report.
O, what a mansion have those vices got
Which for their habitation chose cut thee,
Where beauty's veil doth cover every blot
And all things turns to fair that eyes can see!
    Take heed, dear heart, of this large privilege:
    The hardest knife ill used doth lose his edge.

## 96

Some say thy fault is youth, some wantonness;
Some say thy grace is youth and gentle sport.
Both grace and faults are loved of more and less;
Thou mak'st faults graces that to thee resort.
As on the finger of a thronèd queen
The basest jewel will be well esteemed,
So are those errors that in thee are seen
To truths translated and for true things deemed.
How many lambs might the stern wolf betray
If like a lamb he could his looks translate!
How many gazers mightst thou lead away
If thou wouldst use the strength of all thy state!
    But do not so: I love thee in such sort
    As, thou being mine, mine is thy good report.


## 97

How like a winter hath my absence been
From thee, the pleasure of the fleeting year!
What freezings have I felt, what dark days seen,
What old December's bareness everywhere!
And yet this time removed was summer's time,
The teeming autumn big with rich increase,
Bearing the wanton burden of the prime
Like widowed wombs after their lords' decease.
Yet this abundant issue seemed to me
But hope of orphans and unfathered fruit,
For summer and his pleasures wait on thee,
And thou away, the very birds are mute;
    Or if they sing, 'tis with so dull a cheer
    That leaves look pale, dreading the winter's near.

## 98

From you have I been absent in the spring
When proud-pied April, dressed in all his trim,
Hath put a spirit of youth in everything,
That heavy Saturn laughed and leap'd with him.
Yet nor the lays of birds nor the sweet smell
Of different flowers in odour and in hue
Could make me any summer's story tell,
Or from their proud lap pluck them where they grew;
Nor did I wonder at the lily's white,
Nor praise the deep vermilion in the rose.
They were but sweet, but figures of delight
Drawn after you, you pattern of all those;
    Yet seemed it winter still, and, you away,
    As with your shadow I with these did play.

## 99

The forward violet thus did I chide:
Sweet thief, whence didst thou steal thy sweet that smells,
If not from my love's breath? The purple pride
Which on thy soft cheek for complexion dwells
In my love's veins thou hast too grossly dyed.
The lily I condemnèd for thy hand,
And buds of marjoram had stol'n thy hair;
The roses fearfully on thorns did stand,
One blushing shame, another white despair;
A third, nor red nor white, had stol'n of both,
And to his robb'ry had annexed thy breath;
But for his theft in pride of all his growth
A vengeful canker ate him up to death.
    More flowers I noted, yet I none could see
    But sweet or colour it had stol'n from thee.

## 100

Where art thou, muse, that thou forget'st so long
To speak of that which gives thee all thy might?
Spend'st thou thy fury on some worthless song,
Dark'ning thy power to lend base subjects light?
Return, forgetful muse, and straight redeem
In gentle numbers time so idly spent;
Sing to the ear that doth thy lays esteem
And gives thy pen both skill and argument.
Rise, resty muse, my love's sweet face survey
If time have any wrinkle graven there.
If any, be a satire to decay
And make time's spoils despisèd everywhere.
    Give my love fame faster than time wastes life;
    So, thou prevene'st his scythe and crookèd knife.

## 101

O truant muse, what shall be thy amends
For thy neglect of truth in beauty dyed?
Both truth and beauty on my love depends;
So dost thou too, and therein dignified.
Make answer, muse. Wilt thou not haply say
'Truth needs no colour with his colour fixed,
Beauty no pencil beauty's truth to lay,
But best is best if never intermixed'?
Because he needs no praise wilt thou be dumb?
Excuse not silence so, for't lies in thee
To make him much outlive a gilded tomb,
And to be praised of ages yet to be.
    Then do thy office, muse; I teach thee how
    To make him seem long hence as he shows now.

## 102

My love is strengthened, though more weak in seeming.
I love not less, though less the show appear.
That love is merchandized whose rich esteeming
The owner's tongue doth publish everywhere.
Our love was new and then but in the spring
When I was wont to greet it with my lays,
As Philomel in summer's front doth sing,
And stops her pipe in growth of riper days—
Not that the summer is less pleasant now
Than when her mournful hymns did hush the night,
But that wild music burdens every bough,
And sweets grown common lose their dear delight.
    Therefore like her I sometime hold my tongue,
    Because I would not dull you with my song.

## 103

Alack, what poverty my muse brings forth
That, having such a scope to show her pride,
The argument all bare is of more worth
Than when it hath my added praise beside!
O blame me not if I no more can write!
Look in your glass and there appears a face
That overgoes my blunt invention quite,
Dulling my lines and doing me disgrace.
Were it not sinful then, striving to mend,
To mar the subject that before was well?—
For to no other pass my verses tend
Than of your graces and your gifts to tell;
    And more, much more, than in my verse can sit
    Your own glass shows you when you look in it.

## 104

To me, fair friend, you never can be old;
For as you were when first your eye I eyed,
Such seems your beauty still. Three winters cold
Have from the forests shook three summers' pride;
Three beauteous springs to yellow autumn turned
In process of the seasons have I seen,
Three April perfumes in three hot Junes burned
Since first I saw you fresh, which yet are green.
Ah yet doth beauty, like a dial hand,
Steal from his figure and no pace perceived;
So your sweet hue, which methinks still doth stand,
Hath motion, and mine eye may be deceived.
    For fear of which, hear this, thou age unbred:
    Ere you were born was beauty's summer dead.

## 105

Let not my love be called idolatry,
Nor my belovèd as an idol show,
Since all alike my songs and praises be
To one, of one, still such, and ever so.
Kind is my love today, tomorrow kind,
Still constant in a wondrous excellence.
Therefore my verse, to constancy confined,
One thing expressing, leaves out difference.
'Fair, kind, and true' is all my argument,
'Fair, kind, and true' varying to other words,
And in this change is my invention spent,
Three themes in one, which wondrous scope affords.
    Fair, kind, and true have often lived alone,
    Which three till now never kept seat in one.

106

When in the chronicle of wasted time
I see descriptions of the fairest wights,
And beauty making beautiful old rhyme
In praise of ladies dead and lovely knights;
Then in the blazon of sweet beauty's best,
Of hand, of foot, of lip, of eye, of brow,
I see their antique pen would have expressed
Even such a beauty as you master now.
So all their praises are but prophecies
Of this our time, all you prefiguring,
And for they looked but with divining eyes
They had not skill enough your worth to sing;
　　For we which now behold these present days
　　Have eyes to wonder, but lack tongues to praise.


107

Not mine own fears nor the prophetic soul
Of the wide world dreaming on things to come
Can yet the lease of my true love control,
Supposed as forfeit to a confined doom.
The mortal moon hath her eclipse endured,
And the sad augurs mock their own presage;
Incertainties now crown themselves assured,
And peace proclaims olives of endless age.
Now with the drops of this most balmy time
My love looks fresh, and death to me subscribes,
Since spite of him I'll live in this poor rhyme
While he insults o'er dull and speechless tribes,
　　And thou in this shall find thy monument
　　When tyrants' crests and tombs of brass are spent.

## 108

What's in the brain that ink may character
Which hath not figured to thee my true spirit?
What's new to speak, what new to register,
That may express my love or thy dear merit?
Nothing, sweet boy; but yet like prayers divine
I must each day say o'er the very same,
Counting no old thing old, thou mine, I thine,
Even as when first I hallowed thy fair name.
So that eternal love in love's fresh case
Weighs not the dust and injury of age,
Nor gives to necessary wrinkles place,
But makes antiquity for aye his page,
    Finding the first conceit of love there bred
    Where time and outward form would show it dead.

## 109

O never say that I was false of heart,
Though absence seemed my flame to qualify—
As easy might I from myself depart,
As from my soul, where in thy breast doth lie.
That is my home of love. If I have ranged,
Like him that travels I return again,
Just to the time, not with the time exchanged,
So that myself bring water for my stain.
Never believe, though in my nature reigned
All frailties that besiege all kinds of blood,
That it could so preposterously be stained
To leave for nothing all thy sum of good;
    For nothing this wide universe I call
    Save thou my rose; in it thou art my all.

## 110

Alas, 'tis true, I have gone here and there
And made myself a motley to the view,
Gored mine own thoughts, sold cheap what is most dear,
Made old offences of affections new.
Most true it is that I have looked on truth
Askance and strangely. But, by all above,
These blenches gave my heart another youth,
And worst essays proved thee my best of love
Now all is done, have what shall have no end;
Mine appetite I never more will grind
On newer proof to try an older friend,
A god in love, to whom I am confined.
  Then give me welcome, next my heaven the best,.
  Even to thy pure and most most loving breast.

## 111

O, for my sake do you with fortune chide,
The guilty goddess of my harmful deeds,
That did not better for my life provide
Than public means which public manners breeds.
Thence comes it that my name receives a brand,
And almost thence my nature is subdued
To what it works in, like the dyer's hand.
Pity me then, and wish I were renewed,
Whilst like a willing patient I will drink
Potions of eisel, 'gainst my strong infection;
No bitterness that I will bitter think,
Nor double penance to correct correction.
  Pity me then, dear friend, and I assure ye
  Even that your pity is enough to cure me.

## 112

Your love and pity doth th'impression fill
Which vulgar scandal stamped upon my brow;
For what care I who calls me well or ill,
So you o'er-green my bad, my good allow?
You are my all the world, and I must strive
To know my shames and praises from your tongue—
None else to me, nor I to none alive,
That my steeled sense or changes, right or wrong.
In so profound abyss I throw all care
Of other's voices that my adder's sense
To critic and to flatterer stoppèd are.
Mark how with my neglect I do dispense:
　　You are so strongly in my purpose bred
　　That all the world besides, methinks, are dead.

## 113

Since I left you mine eye is in my mind,
And that which governs me to go about
Doth part his function and is partly blind,
Seems seeing, but effectually is out;
For it no form delivers to the heart
Of bird, of flower, or shape which it doth latch.
Of his quick objects hath the mind no part,
Nor his own vision holds what it doth catch;
For if it see the rud'st or gentlest sight,
The most sweet favour or deformèd'st creature,
The mountain or the sea, the day or night,
The crow or dove, it shapes them to your feature.
　　Incapable of more, replete with you,
　　My most true mind thus maketh mine eye untrue.

## 114

Or whether doth my mind, being crowned with you,
Drink up the monarch's plague, this flattery,
Or whether shall I say mine eye saith true,
And that your love taught it this alchemy,
To make of monsters and things indigest
Such cherubins as your sweet self resemble,
Creating every bad a perfect best
As fast as objects to his beams assemble?
O, 'tis the first, 'tis flatt'ry in my seeing,
And my great mind most kingly drinks it up.
Mine eye well knows what with his gust is 'greeing,
And to his palate doth prepare the cup.
　　If it be poisoned, 'tis the lesser sin
　　That mine eye loves it and doth first begin.

## 115

Those lines that I before have writ do lie,
Even those that said I could not love you dearer;
Yet then my judgement knew no reason why
My most full flame should afterwards burn clearer.
But reckoning time, whose millioned accidents
Creep in 'twixt vows and change decrees of kings,
Tan sacred beauty, blunt the sharpest intents,
Divert strong minds to th' course of alt'ring things—
Alas, why, fearing of time's tyranny,
Might I not then say 'Now I love you best,'
When I was certain o'er uncertainty,
Crowning the present, doubting of the rest?
　　Love is a babe; then might I not say so,
　　To give full growth to that which still doth grow.

## 116

Let me not to the marriage of true minds
Admit impediments. Love is not love
Which alters when it alteration finds,
Or bends with the remover to remove.
O no, it is an ever fixèd mark
That looks on tempests and is never shaken;
It is the star to every wand'ring barque,
Whose worth's unknown although his height be taken.
Love's not time's fool, though rosy lips and cheeks
Within his bending sickle's compass come;
Love alters not with his brief hours and weeks,
But bears it out even to the edge of doom.
　　If this be error and upon me proved,
　　I never writ, nor no man ever loved.

## 117

Accuse me thus: that I have scanted all
Wherein I should your great deserts repay,
Forgot upon your dearest love to call
Whereto all bonds do tie me day by day;
That I have frequent been with unknown minds,
And given to time your own dear-purchased right;
That I have hoisted sail to all the winds
Which should transport me farthest from your sight.
Book both my wilfulness and errors down,
And on just proof surmise accumulate;
Bring me within the level of your frown,
But shoot not at me in your wakened hate,
　　Since my appeal says I did strive to prove
　　The constancy and virtue of your love.

## 118

Like as, to make our appetites more keen,
With eager compounds we our palate urge;
As to prevent our maladies unseen
We sicken to shun sickness when we purge:
Even so, being full of your ne'er cloying sweetness,
To bitter sauces did I frame my feeding,
And, sick of welfare, found a kind of meetness
To be diseased ere that there was true needing.
Thus policy in love, t'anticipate
The ills that were not, grew to faults assured,
And brought to medicine a healthful state
Which, rank of goodness, would by ill be cured.
    But thence I learn, and find the lesson true:
    Drugs poison him that so fell sick of you.

## 119

What potions have I drunk of siren tears
Distilled from limbecks foul as hell within,
Applying fears to hopes and hopes to fears,
Still losing when I saw myself to win!
What wretched errors hath my heart committed
Whilst it hath thought itself so blessèd never!
How have mine eyes out of their spheres been fitted
In the distraction of this madding fever!
O benefit of ill! Now I find true
That better is by evil still made better,
And ruined love when it is built anew
Grows fairer than at first, more strong, far greater.
    So I return rebuked to my content,
    And gain by ills thrice more than I have spent.

## 120

That you were once unkind befriends me now,
And for that sorrow which I then did feel
Needs must I under my transgression bow,
Unless my nerves were brass or hammered steel.
For if you were by my unkindness shaken
As I by yours, you've past a hell of time,
And I, a tyrant, have no leisure taken
To weigh how once I suffered in your crime.
O that our night of woe might have remembered
My deepest sense how hard true sorrow hits,
And soon to you as you to me then tendered
The humble salve which wounded bosoms fits!
　　But that your trespass now becomes a fee;
　　Mine ransoms yours, and yours must ransom me.

## 121

'Tis better to be vile than vile esteemed
When not to be receives reproach of being,
And the just pleasure lost, which is so deemed
Not by our feeling but by others' seeing.
For why should others' false adulterate eyes
Give salutation to my sportive blood?
Or on my frailties why are frailer spies,
Which in their wills count bad what I think good?
No, I am that I am, and they that level
At my abuses reckon up their own.
I may be straight, though they themselves be bevel;
By their rank thoughts my deeds must not be shown,
　　Unless this general evil they maintain:
　　All men are bad and in their badness reign.

## 122

Thy gift, thy tables, are within my brain
Full charactered with lasting memory,
Which shall above that idle rank remain
Beyond all date, even to eternity;
Or at the least so long as brain and heart
Have faculty by nature to subsist,
Till each to razed oblivion yield his part
Of thee, thy record never can be missed.
That poor retention could not so much hold,
Nor need I tallies thy dear love to score;
Therefore to give them from me was I bold,
To trust those tables that receive thee more.
    To keep an adjunct to remember thee
    Were to import forgetfulness in me.

## 123

No, time, thou shalt not boast that I do change!
Thy pyramids built up with newer might
To me are nothing novel, nothing strange,
They are but dressings of a former sight.
Our dates are brief, and therefore we admire
What thou dost foist upon us that is old,
And rather make them born to our desire
Than think that we before have heard them told.
Thy registers and thee I both defy,
Not wond'ring at the present nor the past;
For thy records and what we see do lie,
Made more or less by thy continual haste.
    This I do vow, and this shall ever be:
    I will be true despite thy scythe and thee.

## 124

If my dear love were but the child of state
It might for fortune's bastard be unfathered,
As subject to time's love or to time's hate,
Weeds among weeds or flowers with flowers gathered.
No, it was builded far from accident;
It suffers not in smiling pomp, nor falls
Under the blow of thrallèd discontent
Whereto th'inviting time our fashion calls.
It fears not policy, that heretic
Which works on leases of short-numbered hours,
But all alone stands hugely politic,
That it nor grows with heat nor drowns with showers.
    To this I witness call the fools of time,
      Which die for goodness, who have lived for crime.


## 125

Were't aught to me I bore the canopy,
With my extern the outward honouring,
Or laid great bases for eternity
Which prove more short than waste or ruining?
Have I not seen dwellers on form and favour
Lose all and more by paying too much rent,
For compound sweet foregoing simple savour,
Pitiful thrivers in their gazing spent?
No, let me be obsequious in thy heart,
And take thou my oblation, poor but free,
Which is not mixed with seconds, knows no art
But mutual render, only me for thee.
    Hence, thou suborned informer! A true soul
      When most impeached stands least in thy control.

## 126

O thou my lovely boy, who in thy power
Dost hold time's fickle glass, his sickle-hour;
Who hast by waning grown, and therein show'st
Thy lovers withering as thy sweet self grow'st—
If nature, sovereign mistress over wrack,
As thou goest onwards still will pluck thee back,
She keeps thee to this purpose: that her skill
May time disgrace, and wretched minutes kill.
Yet fear her, O thou minion of her pleasure!
She may detain but not still keep her treasure.
    Her audit, though delayed, answered must be,
    And her quietus is to render thee.

## 127

In the old age black was not counted fair,
Or if it were, it bore not beauty's name;
But now is black beauty's successive heir,
And beauty slandered with a bastard shame:
For since each hand hath put on nature's power,
Fairing the foul with art's false borrowed face,
Sweet beauty hath no name, no holy bower,
But is profaned, if not lives in disgrace.
Therefore my mistress' eyes are raven-black,
Her brow so suited, and they mourners seem
At such who, not born fair, no beauty lack,
Sland'ring creation with a false esteem.
    Yet so they mourn, becoming of their woe,
    That every tongue says beauty should look so.

## 128

How oft, when thou, my music, music play'st
Upon that blessed wood whose motion sounds
With thy sweet fingers when thou gently sway'st
The wiry concord that mine ear confounds,
Do I envy those jacks that nimble leap
To kiss the tender inward of thy hand
Whilst my poor lips, which should that harvest reap,
At the wood's boldness by thee blushing stand!
To be so tickled they would change their state
And situation with those dancing chips
O'er whom thy fingers walk with gentle gait,
Making dead wood more blessed than living lips.
    Since saucy jacks so happy are in this,
    Give them thy fingers, me thy lips to kiss.

## 129

Th'expense of spirit in a waste of shame
Is lust in action; and till action, lust
Is perjured, murd'rous, bloody, full of blame,
Savage, extreme, rude, cruel, not to trust,
Enjoyed no sooner but despisèd straight,
Past reason hunted, and no sooner had
Past reason hated as a swallowed bait,
On purpose laid to make the taker mad;
Mad in pursuit and in possession so,
Had, having, and in quest to have, extreme;
A bliss in proof and proved, a very woe;
Before, a joy proposed; behind, a dream.
    All this the world well knows, yet none knows well
    To shun the heaven that leads men to this hell.

## 130

My mistress' eyes are nothing like the sun;
Coral is far more red than her lips' red.
If snow be white, why then her breasts are dun;
If hairs be wires, black wires grow on her head.
I have seen roses damasked, red and white,
But no such roses see I in her cheeks;
And in some perfumes is there more delight
Than in the breath that from my mistress reeks.
I love to hear her speak, yet well I know
That music hath a far more pleasing sound.
I grant I never saw a goddess go:
My mistress when she walks, treads on the ground.
    And yet, by heaven, I think my love as rare
    As any she belied with false compare.

## 131

Thou art as tyrannous so as thou art
As those whose beauties proudly make them cruel,
For well thou know'st to my dear doting heart
Thou art the fairest and most precious jewel.
Yet, in good faith, some say that thee behold
Thy face hath not the power to make love groan.
To say they err I dare not be so bold,
Although I swear it to myself alone;
And, to be sure that is not false I swear,
A thousand groans but thinking on thy face
One on another's neck, do witness bear
Thy black is fairest in my judgment's place.
    In nothing art thou black save in thy deeds,
    And thence this slander, as I think, proceeds.

## 132

Thine eyes I love, and they, as pitying me—
Knowing thy heart torments me with disdain—
Have put on black, and loving mourners be,
Looking with pretty ruth upon my pain;
And truly, not the morning sun of heaven
Better becomes the gray cheeks of the east,
Nor that full star that ushers in the even
Doth half that glory to the sober west,
As those two mourning eyes become thy face.
O, let it then as well beseem thy heart
To mourn for me, since mourning doth thee grace,
And suit thy pity like in every part.
　　Then will I swear beauty herself is black,
　　And all they foul that thy complexion lack.

## 133

Beshrew that heart that makes my heart to groan
For that deep wound it gives my friend and me!
Is't not enough to torture me alone,
But slave to slavery my sweet'st friend must be?
Me from myself thy cruel eye hath taken,
And my next self thou harder hast engrossed.
Of him, myself, and thee I am forsaken—
A torment thrice threefold thus to be crossed.
Prison my heart in thy steel bosom's ward,
But then my friend's heart let my poor heart bail;
Whoe'er keeps me, let my heart be his guard;
Thou canst not then use rigour in my jail.
　　And yet thou wilt; for I, being pent in thee,
　　Perforce am thine, and all that is in me.

## 134

So, now I have confessed that he is thine,
And I myself am mortgaged to thy will,
Myself I'll forfeit, so that other mine
Thou wilt restore to be my comfort still.
But thou wilt not, nor he will not be free,
For thou art covetous, and he is kind.
He learned but surety-like, to write for me
Under that bond that him as fast doth bind.
The statute of thy beauty thou wilt take,
Thou usurer that putt'st forth all to use,
And sue a friend came debtor for my sake;
So him I lose through my unkind abuse.
    Him have I lost; thou hast both him and me;
    He pays the whole, and yet am I not free.

## 135

Whoever hath her wish, thou hast thy Will,
And Will to boot, and Will in overplus.
More than enough am I that vex thee still,
To thy sweet will making addition thus.
Wilt thou, whose will is large and spacious,
Not once vouchsafe to hide my will in thine?
Shall will in others seem right gracious,
And in my will no fair acceptance shine?
The sea, all water, yet receives rain still,
And in abundance addeth to his store;
So thou, being rich in Will, add to thy Will
One will of mine to make thy large Will more.
    Let no unkind no fair beseechers kill;
    Think all but one, and me in that one Will.

## 136

If thy soul check thee that I come so near,
Swear to thy blind soul that I was thy Will,
And will, thy soul knows, is admitted there;
Thus far for love my love-suit, sweet, fulfil.
Will will fulfil the treasure of thy love,
Ay, fill it full with wills, and my will one.
In things of great receipt with ease we prove
Among a number one is reckoned none.
Then in the number let me pass untold,
Though in thy store's account I one must be;
For nothing hold me, so it please thee hold
That nothing me a something sweet to thee.
    Make but my name thy love, and love that still,
    And then thou lov'st me for my name is Will.

## 137

Thou blind fool love, what dost thou to mine eyes
That they behold and see not what they see?
They know what beauty is, see where it lies,
Yet what the best is take the worst to be.
If eyes corrupt by over-partial looks
Be anchored in the bay where all men ride,
Why of eyes' falsehood hast thou forgèd hooks
Whereto the judgment of my heart is tied?
Why should my heart think that a several plot
Which my heart knows the wide world's common place?—
Or mine eyes, seeing this, say this is not,
To put fair truth upon so foul a face?
    In things right true my heart and eyes have erred,
    And to this false plague are they now transferred.

## 138

When my love swears that she is made of truth
I do believe her though I know she lies,
That she might think me some untutored youth
Unlearnèd in the world's false subtleties
Thus vainly thinking that she thinks me young,
Although she knows my days are past the best,
Simply I credit her false-speaking tongue;
On both sides thus is simple truth suppressed.
But wherefore says she not she is unjust,
And wherefore say not I that I am old?
O, love's best habit is in seeming trust,
And age in love loves not to have years told.
    Therefore I lie with her, and she with me,
    And in our faults by lies we flattered be.

## 139

O, call not me to justify the wrong
That thy unkindness lays upon my heart.
Wound me not with thine eye but with thy tongue;
Use power with power, and slay me not by art.
Tell me thou lov'st elsewhere, but in my sight,
Dear heart, forbear to glance thine eye aside.
What need'st thou wound with cunning when thy might
Is more than my o'erpressed defence can 'bide?
Let me excuse thee: 'Ah! my love well knows
Her pretty looks have been mine enemies,
And therefore from my face she turns my foes
That they elsewhere might dart their injuries.'
    Yet do not so; but since I am near slain,
    Kill me outright with looks, and rid my pain.

## 140

Be wise as thou art cruel; do not press
My tongue-tied patience with too much disdain,
Lest sorrow lend me words, and words express
The manner of my pity-wanting pain.
If I might teach thee wit, better it were,
Though not to love, yet, love, to tell me so—
As testy sick men when their deaths be near
No news but health from their physicians know.
For if I should despair I should grow mad,
And in my madness might speak ill of thee.
Now this ill-wresting world is grown so bad
Mad slanderers by mad ears believèd be.
    That I may not be so, nor thou belied,
    Bear thine eyes straight, though thy proud heart go wide.

## 141

In faith, I do not love thee with mine eyes,
For they in thee a thousand errors note;
But 'tis my heart that loves what they despise,
Who in despite of view is pleased to dote.
Nor are mine ears with thy tongue's tune delighted,
Nor tender feeling to base touches prone;
Nor taste nor smell desire to be invited
To any sensual feast with thee alone;
But my five wits, nor my five senses can
Dissuade one foolish heart from serving thee,
Who leaves unswayed the likeness of a man.
Thy proud heart's slave and vassal-wretch to be.
    Only my plague thus far I count my gain:
    That she that makes me sin awards me pain.

## 142

Love is my sin, and thy dear virtue hate,
Hate of my sin grounded on sinful loving.
O, but with mine compare thou thine own state,
And thou shalt find it merits not reproving;
Or, if it do, not from those lips of thine
That have profaned their scarlet ornaments
And sealed false bonds of love as oft as mine,
Robbed others' beds' revenues of their rents.
Be it lawful I love thee as thou lov'st those
Whom thine eyes woo as mine importune thee.
Root pity in thy heart, that, when it grows
Thy pity may deserve to pitied be.
    If thou dost seek to have what thou dost hide,
    By self example mayst thou be denied!

## 143

Lo, as a care-full housewife runs to catch
One of her feathered creatures broke away,
Sets down her babe and makes all swift dispatch
In pursuit of the thing she would have stay,
Whilst her neglected child holds her in chase,
Cries to catch her whose busy care is bent
To follow that which flies before her face,
Not prizing her poor infant's discontent:
So runn'st thou after that which flies from thee,
Whilst I, thy babe, chase thee afar behind;
But if thou catch thy hope, turn back to me
And play the mother's part: kiss me, be kind.
    So will I pray that thou mayst have thy Will
    If thou turn back and my loud crying still.

## 144

Two loves I have of comfort and despair,
Which like two spirits do suggest me still.
The better angel is a man right fair,
The worser spirit a woman coloured ill.
To win me soon to hell my female evil
Tempteth my better angel from my side,
And would corrupt my saint to be a devil,
Wooing his purity with her foul pride;
And whether that my angel be turned fiend
Suspect I may, yet not directly tell;
But being both from me, both to each friend,
I guess one angel in another's hell.
    Yet this shall I ne'er know, but live in doubt
    Till my bad angel fire my good one out.

## 145

Those lips that love's own hand did make
Breathed forth the sound that said 'I hate'
To me that languished for her sake;
But when she saw my woeful state,
Straight in her heart did mercy come,
Chiding that tongue that ever sweet
Was used in giving gentle doom,
And taught it thus anew to greet:
'I hate' she altered with an end
That followed it as gentle day
Doth follow night who, like a fiend,
From heaven to hell is flown away.
    'I hate' from hate away she threw,
    And saved my life, saying 'not you.'

## 146

Poor soul, the centre of my sinful earth,
] these rebel powers that thee array;
Why dost thou pine within and suffer dearth,
Painting thy outward walls so costly gay?
Why so large cost, having so short a lease,
Dost thou upon thy fading mansion spend?
Shall worms, inheritors of this excess,
Eat up thy charge? Is this thy body's end?
Then, soul, live thou upon thy servant's loss,
And let that pine to aggravate thy store.
Buy terms divine in selling hours of dross;
Within be fed, without be rich no more.
    So shalt thou feed on death, that feeds on men,
    And, Death once dead, there's no more dying then.


## 147

My love is as a fever, longing still
For that which longer nurseth the disease,
Feeding on that which doth preserve the ill,
Th'uncertain sickly appetite to please.
My reason, the physician to my love,
Angry that his prescriptions are not kept,
Hath left me, and I desperate now approve
Desire is death, which physic did except.
Past cure I am, now reason is past care,
And frantic mad with evermore unrest.
My thoughts and my discourse as madmen's are,
At random from the truth vainly expressed;
    For I have sworn thee fair, and thought thee bright,
    Who art as black as hell, as dark as night.

## 148

O me, what eyes hath love put in my head,
Which have no correspondence with true sight!
Or if they have, where is my judgment fled,
That censures falsely what they see aright?
If that be fair whereon my false eyes dote,
What means the world to say it is not so?
If it be not, then love doth well denote
Love's eye is not so true as all men's. No,
How can it, O, how can love's eye be true,
That is so vexed with watching and with tears?
No marvel then though I mistake my view:
The sun itself sees not till heaven clears.
    O cunning love, with tears thou keep'st me blind
    Lest eyes, well seeing, thy foul faults should find!

## 149

Canst thou, O cruel, say I love thee not
When I against myself with thee partake?
Do I not think on thee when I forgot
Am of myself, all-tyrant, for thy sake?
Who hateth thee that I do call my friend?
On whom frown'st thou that I do fawn upon?
Nay, if thou lour'st on me, do I not spend
Revenge upon myself with present moan?
What merit do I in myself respect
That is so proud thy service to despise,
When all my best doth worship thy defect,
Commanded by the motion of thine eyes?
    But, love, hate on; for now I know thy mind.
    Those that can see thou lov'st, and I am blind.

## 150

O, from what power hast thou this powerful might
With insufficiency my heart to sway,
To make me give the lie to my true sight
And swear that brightness doth not grace the day?
Whence hast thou this becoming of things ill,
That in the very refuse of thy deeds
There is such strength and warranties of skill
That in my mind thy worst all best exceeds?
Who taught thee how to make me love thee more
The more I hear and see just cause of hate?
O, though I love what others do abhor,
With others thou shouldst not abhor my state.
    If thy unworthiness raised love in me,
    More worthy I to be beloved of thee.

## 151

Love is too young to know what conscience is,
Yet who knows not conscience is born of love?
Then, gentle cheater, urge not my amiss,
Lest guilty of my faults thy sweet self prove.
For, thou betraying me, I do betray
My nobler part to my gross body's treason.
My soul doth tell my body that he may
Triumph in love; flesh stays no farther reason,
But rising at thy name doth point out thee
As his triumphant prize. Proud of this pride,
He is contented thy poor drudge to be,
To stand in thy affairs, fall by thy side.
    No want of conscience hold it that I call
    Her 'love' for whose dear love I rise and fall.

## 152

In loving thee thou know'st I am forsworn,
But thou art twice forsworn to me love swearing:
In act thy bed-vow broke, and new faith torn
In vowing new hate after new love bearing.
But why of two oaths' breach do I accuse thee
When I break twenty? I am perjured most,
For all my vows are oaths but to misuse thee,
And all my honest faith in thee is lost.
For I have sworn deep oaths of thy deep kindness,
Oaths of thy love, thy truth, thy constancy,
And to enlighten thee gave eyes to blindness,
Or made them swear against the thing they see.
    For I have sworn thee fair—more perjured eye
    To swear against the truth so foul a lie.

## 153

Cupid lay by his brand and fell asleep.
A maid of Dian's this advantage found,
And his love-kindling fire did quickly steep
In a cold valley-fountain of that ground,
Which borrowed from this holy fire of love
A dateless lively heat, still to endure,
And grew a seething bath which yet men prove
Against strange maladies a sovereign cure.
But at my mistress' eye love's brand new fired,
The boy for trial needs would touch my breast.
I, sick withal, the help of bath desired,
And thither hied, a sad distempered guest,
    But found no cure; the bath for my help lies
    Where Cupid got new fire: my mistress' eyes.

## 154

The little love-god lying once asleep
Laid by his side his heart-inflaming brand,
Whilst many nymphs that vowed chaste life to keep
Came tripping by; but in her maiden hand
The fairest votary took up that fire
Which many legions of true hearts had warmed,
And so the general of hot desire
Was sleeping by a virgin hand disarmed.
This brand she quenchèd in a cool well by,
Which from love's fire took heat perpetual,
Growing a bath and healthful remedy
For men diseased; but I, my mistress' thrall,
    Came there for cure, and this by that I prove:
    Love's fire heats water, water cools not love.

# A LOVER'S COMPLAINT

From off a hill whose concave womb re-worded
A plaintful story from a sist'ring vale,
My spirits t'attend this double voice accorded,
And down I laid to list the sad-tuned tale;
Ere long espied a fickle maid full pale,
Tearing of papers, breaking rings a-twain,
Storming her world with sorrow's wind and rain.

Upon her head a plaited hive of straw
Which fortified her visage from the sun,
Whereon the thought might think sometime it saw
The carcass of a beauty spent and done.
Time had not scythèd all that youth begun,
Nor youth all quit; but spite of heaven's fell rage,
Some beauty peeped through lattice of seared age.

Oft did she heave her napkin to her eyne,
Which on it had conceited characters,
Laund'ring the silken figures in the brine
That seasoned woe had pelleted in tears,
And often reading what contents it bears;
As often shrieking undistinguished woe
In clamours of all size, both high and low.

Sometimes her levelled eyes their carriage ride
As they did batt'ry to the spheres intend;
Sometimes diverted their poor balls are tied
To th'orbèd earth; sometimes they do extend
Their view right on; anon their gazes lend
To every place at once, and nowhere fixed,
The mind and sight distractedly commixed.

Her hair, nor loose nor tied in formal plait,
Proclaimed in her a careless hand of pride;
For some, untucked, descended her sheaved hat,
Hanging her pale and pinèd cheek beside.
Some in her threaden fillet still did bide,
And, true to bondage, would not break from thence,
Though slackly braided in loose negligence.

A thousand favours from a maund she drew
Of amber, crystal, and of bedded jet,
Which one by one she in a river threw
Upon whose weeping margin she was set;
Like usury applying wet to wet,
Or monarch's hands that lets not bounty fall
Where want cries some, but where excess begs all.

Of folded schedules had she many a one
Which she perused, sighed, tore, and gave the flood;
Cracked many a ring of posied gold and bone,
Bidding them find their sepulchres in mud;
Found yet more letters sadly penned in blood,
With sleided silk feat and affectedly
Enswathed, and sealed to curious secrecy.

These often bathed she in her fluxive eyes,
And often kissed, and often 'gan to tear;
Cried 'O false blood, thou register of lies,
What unapprovèd witness dost thou bear!
Ink would have seemed more black and damned here!'
This said, in top of rage the lines she rents,
Big discontent so breaking their contents.

A reverend man that grazed his cattle nigh
Sometime a blusterer that the ruffle knew
Of court, of city, and had let go by
The swiftest hours observèd as they flew,
Towards this afflicted fancy fastly drew,
And, privileged by age, desires to know
In brief the grounds and motives of her woe.

So slides he down upon his grainèd bat,
And comely distant sits he by her side,
When he again desires her, being sat,
Her grievance with his hearing to divide.
If that from him there may be aught applied
Which may her suffering ecstasy assuage,
'Tis promised in the charity of age.

'Father,' she says, 'though in me you behold
The injury of many a blasting hour,
Let it not tell your judgment I am old;
Not age, but sorrow over me hath power.
I might as yet have been a spreading flower,
Fresh to myself, if I had self-applied
Love to myself, and to no love beside.

'But, woe is me, too early I attended
A youthful suit—it was to gain my grace—
O, one by nature's outwards so commended
That maidens' eyes stuck over all his face.
Love lacked a dwelling and made him her place,
And when in his fair parts she did abide
She was new-lodged and newly deified.

'His browny locks did hang in crookèd curls,
And every light occasion of the wind
Upon his lips their silken parcels hurls.
What's sweet to do, to do will aptly find.
Each eye that saw him did enchant the mind,
For on his visage was in little drawn
What largeness thinks in paradise was sawn.

'Small show of man was yet upon his chin;
His phoenix down began but to appear,
Like unshorn velvet, on that termless skin
Whose bare outbragged the web it seemed to wear;
Yet showed his visage by that cost more dear,
And nice affections wavering stood in doubt
If best were as it was, or best without.

'His qualities were beauteous as his form,
For maiden-tongued he was, and thereof free.
Yet, if men moved him, was he such a storm
As oft twixt May and April is to see
When winds breathe sweet, unruly though they be.
His rudeness so with his authorized youth
Did livery falseness in a pride of truth.

'Well could he ride, and often men would say
"That horse his mettle from his rider takes;
Proud of subjection, noble by the sway,
What rounds, what bounds, what course, what stop he makes!"
And controversy hence a question takes,
Whether the horse by him became his deed,
Or he his manège by th' well-doing steed.

'But quickly on this side the verdict went:
His real habitude gave life and grace
To appertainings and to ornament,
Accomplished in himself, not in his case.
All aids, themselves made fairer by their place,
Can for additions; yet their purposed trim
Pieced not his grace, but were all graced by him.

'So on the tip of his subduing tongue
All kind of arguments and question deep,
All replication prompt, and reason strong,
For his advantage still did wake and sleep.
To make the weeper laugh, the laugher weep,
He had the dialect and different skill,
Catching all passions in his craft of will,

'That he did in the general bosom reign
Of young, of old, and sexes both enchanted,
To dwell with him in thoughts, or to remain
In personal duty, following where he haunted.
Consents bewitched, ere he desire, have granted,
And dialogued for him what he would say,
Asked their own wills, and made their wills obey.

'Many there were that did his picture get
To serve their eyes, and in it put their mind
Like fools that in th'imagination set
The goodly objects which abroad they find
Of lands and mansions, theirs in thought assigned,
And labour in more pleasures to bestow them
Than the true gouty landlord which doth owe them.

'So many have, that never touched his hand,
Sweetly supposed them mistress of his heart.
My woeful self, that did in freedom stand,
And was my own fee-simple, not in part,
What with his art in youth, and youth in art,
Threw my affections in his charmèd power,
Reserved the stalk and gave him all my flower.

'Yet did I not, as some my equals did,
Demand of him, nor being desired yielded.
Finding myself in honour so forbid,
With safest distance I mine honour shielded.
Experience for me many bulwarks builded
Of proofs new bleeding, which remained the foil
Of this false jewel and his amorous spoil.

'But ah, who ever shunned by precedent
The destined ill she must herself assay,
Or forced examples 'gainst her own content
To put the by-past perils in her way?
Counsel may stop a while what will not stay,
For when we rage, advice is often seen,
By blunting us, to make our wills more keen.

'Nor gives it satisfaction to our blood
That we must curb it upon others' proof,
To be forbod the sweets that seem so good
For fear of harms that preach in our behoof.
O appetite, from judgement stand aloof!
The one a palate hath that needs will taste,
Though reason weep, and cry it is thy last.

'For further I could say this man's untrue,
And knew the patterns of his foul beguiling;
Heard where his plants in others' orchards grew,
Saw how deceits were gilded in his smiling,
Knew vows were ever brokers to defiling,
Thought characters and words merely but art,
And bastards of his foul adulterate heart.

'And long upon these terms I held my city
Till thus he gan besiege me: Gentle maid,
Have of my suffering youth some feeling pity,
And be not of my holy vows afraid.
That's to ye sworn to none was ever said;
For feasts of love I have been called unto,
Till now did ne'er invite nor never woo.

' "All my offences that abroad you see
Are errors of the blood, none of the mind.
Love made them not; with acture they may be,
Where neither party is nor true nor kind.
They sought their shame that so their shame did find.
And so much less of shame in me remains
By how much of me their reproach contains.

' "Among the many that mine eyes have seen,
Not one whose flame my heart so much as warmèd
On my affection put to th' smallest teen,
Or any of my leisures ever charmèd.
Harm have I done to them, but ne'er was harmèd;
Kept hearts in liveries, but mine own was free,
And reigned commanding in his monarchy.

' "Look here what tributes wounded fancies sent me
Of pallid pearls and rubies red as blood,
Figuring that they their passions likewise lent me
Of grief and blushes, aptly understood
In bloodless white and the encrimsoned mood—
Effects of terror and dear modesty,
Encamped in hearts, but fighting outwardly.

‘ "And lo, behold, the talents of their hair,
With twisted mettle amorously impleached,
I have received from many a several fair,
Their kind acceptance weepingly beseeched,
With th'annexations of fair gems enriched,
And deep-brained sonnets that did amplify
Each stone's dear nature, worth, and quality.

‘ "The diamond?—why, 'twas beautiful and hard,
Whereto his invised properties did tend;
The deep-green em'rald, in whose fresh regard
Weak sights their sickly radiance do amend;
The heaven-hued sapphire and the opal blend
With objects manifold; each several stone,
With wit well blazoned, smiled or made some moan.

‘ "Lo, all these trophies of affections hot,
Of pensived and subdued desires the tender,
Nature hath charged me that I hoard them not,
But yield them up where I myself must render—
That is to you, my origin and ender;
For these of force must your oblations be,
Since I their altar, you enpatron me.

‘ "O then advance of yours that phraseless hand
Whose white weighs down the airy scale of praise.
Take all these similes to your own command,
Hallowed with sighs that burning lungs did raise.
What me, your minister for you, obeys,
Works under you, and to your audit comes
Their distract parcels in combinèd sums.

‘ "Lo, this device was sent me from a nun,
A sister sanctified of holiest note,
Which late her noble suit in court did shun,
Whose rarest havings made the blossoms dote;
For she was sought by spirits of richest coat,
But kept cold distance, and did thence remove
To spend her living in eternal love.

' "But O, my sweet, what labour is't to leave
The thing we have not, mast'ring what not strives,
Planing the place which did no form receive,
Playing patient sports in unconstrainèd gyves!
She that her fame so to herself contrives
The scars of battle scapeth by the flight,
And makes her absence valiant, not her might.

' "O, pardon me, in that my boast is true!
The accident which brought me to her eye
Upon the moment did her force subdue,
And now she would the cagèd cloister fly.
Religious love put out religion's eye.
Not to be tempted would she be immured,
And now, to tempt, all liberty procured.

' "How mighty then you are, O hear me tell!
The broken bosoms that to me belong
Have emptied all their fountains in my well,
And mine I pour your ocean all among.
I strong o'er them, and you o'er me being strong,
Must for your victory us all congest,
As compound love to physic your cold breast.

' "My parts had power to charm a sacred nun,
Who disciplined, ay dieted in grace,
Believed her eyes when they t' assail begun,
All vows and consecrations giving place.
O most potential love: vow, bond, nor space
In thee hath neither sting, knot, nor confine,
For thou art all, and all things else are thine.

' "When thou impressest, what are precepts worth
Of stale example? When thou wilt inflame,
How coldly those impediments stand forth
Of wealth, of filial fear, law, kindred, fame.
Love's arms are peace, 'gainst rule, 'gainst sense, 'gainst shame;
And sweetens in the suff'ring pangs it bears
The aloes of all forces, shocks, and fears.

' "Now all these hearts that do on mine depend,
Feeling it break, with bleeding groans they pine,
And supplicant their sighs to you extend,
To leave the battery that you make 'gainst mine,
Lending soft audience to my sweet design,
And credent soul to that strong-bonded oath,
That shall prefer and undertake my troth."

'This said, his wat'ry eyes he did dismount,
Whose sights till then were levelled on my face.
Each cheek a river running from a fount
With brinish current downward flowed apace.
O, how the channel to the stream gave grace,
Who, glazed with crystal gate the glowing roses
That flame through water which their hue encloses.

'O father, what a hell of witchcraft lies
In the small orb of one particular tear!
But with the inundation of the eyes
What rocky heart to water will not wear?
What breast so cold that is not warmèd here?
O cleft effect! Cold modesty, hot wrath,
Both fire from hence and chill extincture hath.

'For lo, his passion, but an art of craft,
Even there resolved my reason into tears.
There my white stole of chastity I daffed,
Shook off my sober guards and civil fears;
Appear to him as he to me appears,
All melting, though our drops this diff'rence bore:
His poisoned me, and mine did him restore.

'In him a plenitude of subtle matter,
Applied to cautels, all strange forms receives,
Of burning blushes or of weeping water,
Or swooning paleness; and he takes and leaves,
In either's aptness, as it best deceives,
To blush at speeches rank, to weep at woes,
Or to turn white and swoon at tragic shows,

'That not a heart which in his level came
Could scape the hail of his all-hurting aim,
Showing fair nature is both kind and tame,
And, veiled in them, did win whom he would maim.
Against the thing he sought he would exclaim;
When he most burned in heart-wished luxury,
He preached pure maid and praised cold chastity.

'Thus merely with the garment of a grace
The naked and concealèd fiend he covered,
That th'unexperient gave the tempter place,
Which like a cherubin above them hovered.
Who, young and simple, would not be so lovered?
Ah me, I fell, and yet do question make
What I should do again for such a sake.

'O that infected moisture of his eye,
O that false fire which in his cheek so glowed,
O that forced thunder from his heart did fly,
O that sad breath his spongy lungs bestowed,
O all that borrowed motion seeming owed
Would yet again betray the fore-betrayed,
And new pervert a reconcilèd maid.'

# VENUS AND ADONIS

*Vilia miretur vulgus; mihi flavus Apollo*
*Pocula Castalia plena ministret aqua.*

To the Right Honourable Henry Wriothesley,
Earl of Southampton, and Baron of Titchfield

Right Honourable, I know not how I shall offend in dedicating my unpolished lines to your lordship, nor how the world will censure me for choosing so strong a prop to support so weak a burden.

Only, if your honour seem but pleased, I account myself highly praised, and vow to take advantage of all idle hours till I have honoured you with some graver labour. But if the first heir of my invention prove deformed, I shall be sorry it had so noble a godfather, and never after ear so barren a land for fear it yield me still so bad a harvest. I leave it to your honourable survey, and your honour to your heart's content, which I wish may always answer your own wish and the world's hopeful expectation. Your honour's in all duty,

William Shakespeare

Even as the sun with purple-coloured face
Had ta'en his last leave of the weeping morn,
Rose-cheeked Adonis hied him to the chase.
Hunting he loved, but love he laughed to scorn;
    Sick-thoughted Venus makes amain unto him,
    And like a bold-faced suitor 'gins to woo him.

'Thrice fairer than myself,' thus she began,
'The field's chief flower, sweet above compare,
Stain to all nymphs, more lovely than a man,
More white and red than doves or roses are—
    Nature that made thee with herself at strife
    Saith that the world hath ending with thy life.

'Vouchsafe, thou wonder, to alight thy steed
And rein his proud head to the saddle-bow;
If thou wilt deign this favour, for thy meed
A thousand honey secrets shalt thou know.
    Here come and sit where never serpent hisses;
    And being sat, I'll smother thee with kisses,

'And yet not cloy thy lips with loathed satiety,
But rather famish them amid their plenty,
Making them red and pale, with fresh variety;
Ten kisses short as one, one long as twenty.
    A summer's day will seem an hour but short,
    Being wasted in such time-beguiling sport.'

With this, she seizeth on his sweating palm,
The precedent of pith and livelihood,
And, trembling in her passion, calls it balm—
Earth's sovereign salve to do a goddess good.
    Being so enraged, desire doth lend her force
    Courageously to pluck him from his horse.

Over one arm, the lusty courser's rein;
Under her other was the tender boy,
Who blushed and pouted in a dull disdain
With leaden appetite, unapt to toy.
    She red and hot as coals of glowing fire;
    He red for shame, but frosty in desire.

The studded bridle on a ragged bough
Nimbly she fastens—O, how quick is love!
The steed is stallèd up, and even now
To tie the rider she begins to prove.
    Backward she pushed him, as she would be thrust,
    And governed him in strength, though not in lust.

So soon was she along as he was down,
Each leaning on their elbows and their hips.
Now doth she stroke his cheek, now doth he frown
And 'gins to chide, but soon she stops his lips,
    And, kissing, speaks, with lustful language broken:
    'If thou wilt chide, thy lips shall never open.'

He burns with bashful shame; she with her tears
Doth quench the maiden burning of his cheeks.
Then, with her windy sighs and golden hairs,
To fan and blow them dry again she seeks.
    He saith she is immodest, blames her miss;
    What follows more she murders with a kiss.

Even as an empty eagle, sharp by fast,
Tires with her beak on feathers, flesh, and bone,
Shaking her wings, devouring all in haste
Till either gorge be stuffed or prey be gone,
    Even so she kissed his brow, his cheek, his chin,
    And where she ends she doth anew begin.

Forced to content, but never to obey,
Panting he lies and breatheth in her face.
She feedeth on the steam as on a prey
And calls it heavenly moisture, air of grace,
    Wishing her cheeks were gardens full of flowers,
    So they were dewed with such distilling showers.

Look how a bird lies tangled in a net,
So fastened in her arms Adonis lies.
Pure shame and awed resistance made him fret,
Which bred more beauty in his angry eyes.
    Rain added to a river that is rank
    Perforce will force it overflow the bank.

Still she entreats, and prettily entreats,
For to a pretty ear she tunes her tale.
Still is he sullen, still he lours and frets
'Twixt crimson shame and anger ashy-pale.
    Being red she loves him best; and being white,
    Her best is bettered with a more delight.

Look how he can, she cannot choose but love;
And by her fair immortal hand she swears
From his soft bosom never to remove
Till he take truce with her contending tears,
    Which long have rained, making her cheeks all wet;
    And one sweet kiss shall pay this countless debt.

Upon this promise did he raise his chin,
Like a divedapper peering through a wave
Who, being looked on, ducks as quickly in—
So offers he to give what she did crave.
    But when her lips were ready for his pay,
    He winks, and turns his lips another way.

Never did passenger in summer's heat
More thirst for drink than she for this good turn.
Her help she sees, but help she cannot get.
She bathes in water, yet her fire must burn.
    'O pity,' gan she cry, 'flint-hearted boy!
    'Tis but a kiss I beg—why art thou coy?

'I have been wooed as I entreat thee now
Even by the stern and direful god of war,
Whose sinewy neck in battle ne'er did bow,
Who conquers where he comes in every jar.
　　Yet hath he been my captive and my slave,
　　And begged for that which thou unasked shalt have.

'Over my altars hath he hung his lance,
His battered shield, his uncontrollèd crest,
And for my sake hath learned to sport and dance,
To toy, to wanton, dally, smile, and jest,
　　Scorning his churlish drum and ensign red,
　　Making my arms his field, his tent my bed.

'Thus he that over-ruled I overswayed,
Leading him prisoner in a red-rose chain.
Strong-tempered steel his stronger strength obeyed,
Yet was he servile to my coy disdain.
　　O, be not proud, nor brag not of thy might,
　　For mast'ring her that foiled the god of fight.

'Touch but my lips with those fair lips of thine—
Though mine be not so fair, yet are they red—
The kiss shall be thine own as well as mine.
What seest thou in the ground? Hold up thy head.
　　Look in mine eyeballs: there thy beauty lies.
　　Then why not lips on lips, since eyes in eyes?

'Art thou ashamed to kiss? Then wink again,
And I will wink. So shall the day seem night.
Love keeps his revels where there are but twain.
Be bold to play—our sport is not in sight.
　　These blue-veined violets whereon we lean
　　Never can blab, nor know not what we mean.

'The tender spring upon thy tempting lip
Shows thee unripe: yet mayst thou well be tasted.
Make use of time; let not advantage slip.
Beauty within itself should not be wasted.
    Fair flowers that are not gathered in their prime
    Rot, and consume themselves in little time.

'Were I hard-favoured, foul, or wrinkled-old,
Ill-nurtured, crooked, churlish, harsh in voice,
O'er-worn, despisèd, rheumatic, and cold,
Thick-sighted, barren, lean, and lacking juice,
    Then mightst thou pause, for then I were not for thee.
    But having no defects, why dost abhor me?

'Thou canst not see one winkle in my brow.
Mine eyes are grey, and bright, and quick in turning.
My beauty as the spring doth yearly grow.
My flesh is soft and plump, my marrow burning.
    My smooth moist hand, were it with thy hand felt,
    Would in thy palm dissolve, or seem to melt.

'Bid me discourse, I will enchant thine ear;
Or like a fairy, trip upon the green;
Or like a nymph, with long, dishevelled hair,
Dance on the sands, and yet no footing seen.
    Love is a spirit all compact of fire,
    Not gross to sink, but light, and will aspire.

'Witness this primrose bank whereon I lie:
These forceless flowers like sturdy trees support me.
Two strengthless doves will draw me through the sky
From morn till night, even where I list to sport me.
    Is love so light, sweet boy, and may it be
    That thou should think it heavy unto thee?

'Is thine own heart to thine own face affected?
Can thy right hand seize love upon thy left?
Then woo thyself, be of thyself rejected;
Steal thine own freedom, and complain on theft.
    Narcissus so himself himself forsook,
    And died to kiss his shadow in the brook.

'Torches are made to light, jewels to wear,
Dainties to taste, fresh beauty for the use,
Herbs for their smell, and sappy plants to bear.
Things growing to themselves are growth's abuse.
    Seeds spring from seeds, and beauty breedeth beauty:
    Thou wast begot; to get it is thy duty.

'Upon the earth's increase why shouldst thou feed
Unless the earth with thy increase be fed?
By law of nature thou art bound to breed,
That thine may live when thou thyself art dead;
    And so in spite of death thou dost survive,
    In that thy likeness still is left alive.'

By this, the lovesick queen began to sweat,
For where they lay the shadow had forsook them,
And Titan, tired in the midday heat,
With burning eye did hotly overlook them,
    Wishing Adonis had his team to guide
    So he were like him, and by Venus' side.

And now Adonis, with a lazy sprite
And with a heavy, dark, disliking eye,
His louring brows o'erwhelming his fair sight,
Like misty vapours when they blot the sky,
    Souring his cheeks, cries, 'Fie, no more of love!
    The sun doth burn my face; I must remove.'

'Ay me,' quoth Venus, 'young, and so unkind?
What bare excuses mak'st thou to be gone?
I'll sigh celestial breath, whose gentle wind
Shall cool the heat of this descending sun.
    I'll make a shadow for thee of my hairs;
    If they burn too, I'll quench them with my tears.

'The sun that shines from heaven shines but warm,
And lo, I lie between that sun and thee.
The heat I have from thence doth little harm;
Thine eye darts forth the fire that burneth me,
    And were I not immortal, life were done
    Between this heavenly and earthly sun.

'Art thou obdurate, flinty, hard as steel?
Nay, more than flint, for stone at rain relenteth.
Art thou a woman's son, and canst not feel
What 'tis to love, how want of love tormenteth?
    O, had thy mother borne so hard a mind,
    She had not brought forth thee, but died unkind.

'What am I, that thou shouldst contemn me this?
Or what great danger dwells upon my suit?
What were thy lips the worse for one poor kiss?
Speak, fair; but speak fair words, or else be mute.
    Give me one kiss, I'll give it thee again,
    And one for int'rest if thou wilt have twain.

'Fie, lifeless picture, cold and senseless stone,
Well painted idol, image dull and dead,
Statue contenting but the eye alone,
Thing like a man, but of no woman bred:
    Thou art no man, though of a man's complexion,
    For men will kiss even by their own direction.'

This said, impatience chokes her pleading tongue,
And swelling passion doth provoke a pause.
Red cheeks and fiery eyes blaze forth her wrong.
Being judge in love, she cannot right her cause;
    And now she weeps, and now she fain would speak,
    And now her sobs do her intendments break.

Sometimes she shakes her head, and then his hand;
Now gazeth she on him, now on the ground.
Sometimes her arms enfold him like a band;
She would, he will not in her arms be bound.
    And when from thence he struggles to be gone,
    She locks her lily fingers one in one.

'Fondling,' she saith, 'since I have hemmed thee here
Within the circuit of this ivory pale,
I'll be a park, and thou shalt be my deer.
Feed where thou wilt, on mountain or in dale;
    Graze on my lips, and if those hills be dry,
    Stray lower, where the pleasant fountains lie.

'Within this limit is relief enough,
Sweet bottom-grass, and high delightful plain,
Round rising hillocks, brakes obscure and rough,
To shelter thee from tempest and from rain.
    Then be my deer, since I am such a park;
    No dog shall rouse thee, though a thousand bark.'

At this Adonis smiles as in disdain,
That in each cheek appears a pretty dimple.
Love made those hollows, if himself were slain,
He might be buried in a tomb so simple,
    Foreknowing well, if there he came to lie,
    Why, there love lived, and there he could not die.

These lovely caves, these round enchanting pits,
Opened their mouths to swallow Venus' liking.
Being mad before, how doth she now for wits?
Struck dead at first, what needs a second striking?
    Poor queen of love, in thine own law forlorn,
    To love a cheek that smiles at thee in scorn!

Now which way shall she turn? What shall she say?
Her words are done, her woes the more increasing.
The time is spent; her object will away,
And from her twining arms doth urge releasing.
    'Pity,' she cries; 'some favour, some remorse!'
    Away he springs, and hasteth to his horse.

But lo, from forth a copse that neighbours by
A breeding jennet, lusty, young, and proud,
Adonis' tramping courser doth espy,
And forth she rushes, snorts, and neighs aloud.
    The strong-necked steed, being tied unto a tree,
    Breaketh his rein, and to her straight goes he.

Imperiously he leaps, he neighs, he bounds,
And now his woven girths he breaks asunder.
The bearing earth with his hard hoof he wounds,
Whose hollow womb resounds like heaven's thunder.
    The iron bit he crusheth 'tween his teeth,
    Controlling what he was controllèd with.

His ears up-pricked, his braided hanging mane
Upon his compassed crest now stand on end;
His nostrils drink the air, and forth again,
As from a furnace, vapours doth he send.
    His eye, which scornfully glisters like fire,
    Shows his hot courage and his high desire.

Sometime he trots, as if he told the steps,
With gentle majesty and modest pride.
Anon he rears upright, curvets and leaps,
As who should say, 'Lo, thus my strength is tried,
    And this I do to captivate the eye
    Of the fair breeder that is standing by.'

What recketh he his rider's angry stir,
His flattering 'Holla,' or his 'Stand, I say'?
What cares he now for curb or pricking spur,
For rich caparisons or trappings gay?
    He sees his love, and nothing else he sees,
    Nor nothing else with his proud sight agrees.

Look when a painter would surpass the life
In limning out a well proportioned steed,
His art with nature's workmanship at strife,
As if the dead the living should exceed:
    So did this horse excel a common one
    In shape, in courage, colour, pace, and bone.

Round-hoofed, short-jointed, fetlocks shag and long,
Broad breast, full eye, small head, and nostril wide,
High crest, short ears, straight legs, and passing strong;
Thin mane, thick tail, broad buttock, tender hide—
    Look what a horse should have he did not lack,
    Save a proud rider on so proud a back.

Sometimes he scuds far off, and there he stares;
Anon he starts at stirring of a feather.
To bid the wind a base he now prepares,
And whe'er he run or fly they know not whether;
    For through his mane and tail the high wind sings,
    Fanning the hairs, who wave like feathered wings.

He looks upon his love, and neighs unto her;
She answers him as if she knew his mind.
Being proud, as females are, to see him woo her,
She puts on outward strangeness, seems unkind,
 Spurns at his love, and scorns the heat he feels,
 Beating his kind embracements with her heels.

Then, like a melancholy malcontent,
He vails his tail that, like a falling plume,
Cool shadow to his melting buttock lent.
He stamps, and bites the poor flies in his fume.
 His love, perceiving how he was enraged,
 Grew kinder, and his fury was assuaged.

His testy master goeth about to take him,
When lo! the unbacked breeder, full of fear,
Jealous of catching, swiftly doth forsake him,
With her the horse, and left Adonis there.
 As they were mad unto the wood they hie them,
 Outstripping crows that strive to overfly them.

All swoll'n with chafing, down Adonis sits,
Banning his boist'rous and unruly beast;
And now the happy season once more fits
That love-sick love by pleading may be blessed;
 For lovers say the heart hath treble wrong
 When it is barred the aidance of the tongue.

An oven that is stopped, or river stayed,
Burneth more hotly, swelleth with more rage.
So of concealèd sorrow may be said
Free vent of words love's fire doth assuage.
 But when the heart's attorney once is mute,
 The client breaks, as desperate in his suit.

He sees her coming, and begins to glow,
Even as a dying coal revives with wind,
And with his bonnet hides his angry brow,
Looks on the dull earth with disturbèd mind,
Taking no notice that she is so nigh,
For all askance he holds her in his eye.

O, what a sight it was wistly to view
How she came stealing to the wayward boy,
To note the fighting conflict of her hue,
How white and red each other did destroy!
But now her cheek was pale; and by and by
It flashed forth fire, as lightning from the sky.

Now was she just before him as he sat,
And like a lowly lover down she kneels;
With one fair hand she heaveth up his hat;
Her other tender hand his fair cheek feels.
His tend'rer cheek receives her soft hand's print
As apt as new-fall'n snow takes any dint.

O, what a war of looks was then between them,
Her eyes petitioners to his eyes suing!
His eyes saw her eyes as they had not seen them;
Her eyes wooed still; his eyes disdained the wooing;
And all this dumb play had his acts made plain
With tears which, chorus-like, her eyes did rain.

Full gently now she takes him by the hand,
A lily prisoned in a jail of snow,
Or ivory in an alabaster band;
So white a friend engirds so white a foe.
This beauteous combat, wilful and unwilling,
Showed like two silver doves that sit a-billing.

Once more the engine of her thoughts began:
'O fairest mover on this mortal round,
Would thou wert as I am, and I a man,
My heart all whole as thine, thy heart my wound;
    For one sweet look thy help I would assure thee,
    Though nothing but my body's bane would cure thee.'

'Give me my hand,' saith he. 'Why dost thou feel it?'
'Give me my heart,' saith she, 'and thou shalt have it.
O, give it me, lest thy hard heart do steel it,
And, being steeled, soft sighs can never grave it;
    Then love's deep groans I never shall regard,
    Because Adonis' heart hath made mine hard.'

'For shame,' he cries, 'let go, and let me go!
My day's delight is past; my horse is gone,
And 'tis your fault I am bereft him so.
I pray you hence, and leave me here alone;
    For all my mind, my thought, my busy care
    Is how to get my palfrey from the mare.'

Thus she replies: 'Thy palfrey, as he should,
Welcomes the warm approach of sweet desire.
Affection is a coal that must be cooled,
Else, suffered, it will set the heart on fire.
    The sea hath bounds, but deep desire hath none;
    Therefore no marvel though thy horse be gone.

'How like a jade he stood tied to the tree,
Servilely mastered with a leathern rein!
But when he saw his love, his youth's fair fee,
He held such petty bondage in disdain,
    Throwing the base thong from his bending crest,
    Enfranchising his mouth, his back, his breast.

'Who sees his true-love in her naked bed,
Teaching the sheets a whiter hue than white,
But when his glutton eye so full hath fed
His other agents aim at like delight?
    Who is so faint that dare not be so bold
    To touch the fire, the weather being cold?

'Let me excuse thy courser, gentle boy;
And learn of him, I heartily beseech thee,
To take advantage on presented joy
Though I were dumb, yet his proceedings teach thee.
    O, learn to love! The lesson is but plain,
    And once made perfect, never lost again.'

'I know not love,' quoth he, 'nor will not know it,
Unless it be a boar, and then I chase it.
'Tis much to borrow, and I will not owe it.
My love to love is love but to disgrace it;
    For I have heard it is a life in death,
    That laughs and weeps, and all but with a breath.

'Who wears a garment shapeless and unfinished?
Who plucks the bud before one leaf put forth?
If springing things be any jot diminished,
They wither in their prime, prove nothing worth.
    The colt that's backed and burdened being young,
    Loseth his pride, and never waxeth strong.

'You hurt my hand with wringing. Let us part,
And leave this idle theme, this bootless chat.
Remove your siege from my unyielding heart;
To love's alarms it will not ope the gate.
    Dismiss your vows, your feignèd tears, your flatt'ry;
    For where a heart is hard they make no batt'ry.'

'What, canst thou talk?' quoth she. 'Hast thou a tongue?
O, would thou hadst not, or I had no hearing!
Thy mermaid's voice hath done me double wrong.
I had my load before, now pressed with bearing:
    Melodious discord, heavenly tune harsh sounding,
    Ear's deep-sweet music, and heart's deep-sore wounding.

'Had I no eyes but ears, my ears would love
That inward beauty and invisible;
Or were I deaf, thy outward parts would move
Each part in me that were but sensible.
    Though neither eyes nor ears to hear nor see,
    Yet should I be in love by touching thee.

'Say that the sense of feeling were bereft me,
And that I could not see, nor hear, nor touch,
And nothing but the very smell were left me,
Yet would my love to thee be still as much;
    For from the stillitory of thy face excelling
    Comes breath perfumed, that breedeth love by smelling.

'But O, what banquet wert thou to the taste,
Being nurse and feeder of the other four!
Would they not wish the feast might ever last
And bid suspicion double-lock the door
    Lest jealousy, that sour unwelcome guest,
    Should by his stealing-in disturb the feast?'

Once more the ruby-coloured portal opened,
Which to his speech did honey passage yield,
Like a red morn that ever yet betokened
Wrack to the seaman, tempest to the field,
    Sorrow to shepherds, woe unto the birds,
    Gusts and foul flaws to herdmen and to herds.

This ill presage advisedly she marketh.
Even as the wind is hushed before it raineth,
Or as the wolf doth grin before he barketh,
Or as the berry breaks before it staineth,
    Or like the deadly bullet of a gun,
     His meaning struck her ere his words begun,

And at his look she flatly falleth down,
For looks kill love, and love by looks reviveth;
A smile recures the wounding of a frown,
But blessèd bankrupt that by loss so thriveth!
    The silly boy, believing she is dead,
     Claps her pale cheek till clapping makes it red,

And, all amazed, brake off his late intent,
For sharply he did think to reprehend her,
Which cunning love did wittily prevent.
Fair fall the wit that can so well defend her!
    For on the grass she lies as she were slain,
     Till his breath breatheth life in her again.

He wrings her nose, he strikes her on the cheeks,
He bends her fingers, holds her pulses hard;
He chafes her lips; a thousand ways he seeks
To mend the hurt that his unkindness marred.
    He kisses her; and she, by her good will,
     Will never rise, so he will kiss her still.

The night of sorrow now is turned to day.
Her two blue windows faintly she up heaveth,
Like the fair sun when, in his fresh array,
He cheers the morn, and all the world relieveth;
    And as the bright sun glorifies the sky,
     So is her face illumined with her eye,

Whose beams upon his hairless face are fixed,
As if from thence they borrowed all their shine.
Were never four such lamps together mixed,
Had not his clouded with his brow's repine.
    But hers, which through the crystal tears gave light,
    Shone like the moon in water seen by night.

'O, where am I?' quoth she; 'in earth or heaven,
Or in the ocean drenched, or in the fire?
What hour is this: or morn or weary even?
Do I delight to die, or life desire?
    But now I lived, and life was death's annoy;
    But now I died, and death was lively joy.

'O, thou didst kill me; kill me once again!
Thy eyes' shrewd tutor, that hard heart of thine,
Hath taught them scornful tricks, and such disdain
That they have murdered this poor heart of mine,
    And these mine eyes, true leaders to their queen,
    But for thy piteous lips no more had seen.

'Long may they kiss each other, for this cure!
O, never let their crimson liveries wear,
And as they last, their verdure still endure
To drive infection from the dangerous year,
    That the star-gazers, having writ on death,
    May say the plague is banished by thy breath!

'Pure lips, sweet seals in my soft lips imprinted,
What bargains may I make still to be sealing?
To sell myself I can be well contented,
So thou wilt buy, and pay, and use good dealing;
    Which purchase if thou make, for fear of slips
    Set thy seal manual on my wax-red lips.

'A thousand kisses buys my heart from me;
And pay them at thy leisure, one by one.
What is ten hundred touches unto thee?
Are they not quickly told, and quickly gone?
 Say for non-payment that the debt should double,
 Is twenty hundred kisses such a trouble?'

'Fair queen,' quoth he, 'if any love you owe me,
Measure my strangeness with my unripe years.
Before I know myself, seek not to know me.
No fisher but the ungrown fry forbears.
 The mellow plum doth fall, the green sticks fast,
 Or, being early plucked, is sour to taste.

'Look, the world's comforter with weary gait
His day's hot task hath ended in the west.
The owl, night's herald, shrieks 'tis very late;
The sheep are gone to fold, birds to their nest,
 And coal-black clouds, that shadow heaven's light,
 Do summon us to part and bid good night.

'Now let me say good night, and so say you.
If you will say so, you shall have a kiss.'
'Good night,' quoth she; and ere he says adieu
The honey fee of parting tendered is.
 Her arms do lend his neck a sweet embrace.
 Incorporate then they seem; face grows to face,

Till breathless he disjoined, and backward drew
The heavenly moisture, that sweet coral mouth,
Whose precious taste her thirsty lips well knew,
Whereon they surfeit, yet complain on drouth.
 He with her plenty pressed, she faint with dearth,
 Their lips together glued, fall to the earth.

Now quick desire hath caught the yielding prey,
And glutton-like she feeds, yet never filleth.
Her lips are conquerors, his lips obey,
Paying what ransom the insulter willeth,
    Whose vulture thought doth pitch the price so high,
    That she will draw his lips' rich treasure dry,

And, having felt the sweetness of the spoil,
With blindfold fury she begins to forage.
Her face doth reek and smoke, her blood doth boil,
And careless lust stirs up a desperate courage,
    Planting oblivion, beating reason back,
    Forgetting shame's pure blush and honour's wrack.

Hot, faint, and weary with her hard embracing,
Like a wild bird being tamed with too much handling,
Or as the fleet-foot roe that's tired with chasing,
Or like the froward infant stilled with dandling,
    He now obeys, and now no more resisteth,
    While she takes all she can, not all she listeth.

What wax so frozen but dissolves with temp'ring
And yields at last to every light impression?
Things out of hope are compassed oft with vent'ring,
Chiefly in love, whose leave exceeds commission.
    Affection faints not, like a pale-faced coward,
    But then woos best when most his choice is froward.

When he did frown, O, had she then gave over,
Such nectar from his lips she had not sucked.
Foul words and frowns must not repel a lover.
What though the rose have prickles, yet 'tis plucked!
    Were beauty under twenty locks kept fast,
    Yet love breaks through, and picks them all at last.

For pity now she can no more detain him.
The poor fool prays her that he may depart.
She is resolved no longer to restrain him,
Bids him farewell, and look well to her heart,
    The which, by Cupid's bow she doth protest,
    He carries thence incagèd in his breast.

'Sweet boy,' she says, 'this night I'll waste in sorrow,
For my sick heart commands mine eyes to watch.
Tell me, love's master, shall we meet tomorrow?
Say, shall we, shall we? Wilt thou make the match?'
    He tells her no, tomorrow he intends
    To hunt the boar with certain of his friends.

'The boar!' quoth she; whereat a sudden pale,
Like lawn being spread upon the blushing rose,
Usurps her cheek. She trembles at his tale,
And on his neck her yoking arms she throws.
    She sinketh down, still hanging by his neck.
    He on her belly falls, she on her back.

Now is she in the very lists of love,
Her champion mounted for the hot encounter.
All is imaginary she doth prove.
He will not manage her, although he mount her,
    That worse than Tantalus' is her annoy,
    To clip Elysium, and to lack her joy.

Even as poor birds, deceived with painted grapes,
Do surfeit by the eye, and pine the maw;
Even so she languisheth in her mishaps
As those poor birds that helpless berries saw.
    The warm effects which she in him finds missing
    She seeks to kindle with continual kissing.

But all in vain, good queen! It will not be.
She hath assayed as much as may be proved;
Her pleading hath deserved a greater fee:
She's Love; she loves; and yet she is not loved.
    'Fie, fie,' he says, 'you crush me. Let me go.
    You have no reason to withhold me so.'

'Thou hadst been gone,' quoth she, 'sweet boy, ere this,
But that thou told'st me thou wouldst hunt the boar.
O, be advised; thou know'st not what it is
With javelin's point a churlish swine to gore,
    Whose tushes, never sheathed, he whetteth still,
    Like to a mortal butcher, bent to kill.

'On his bow-back he hath a battle set
Of bristly pikes that ever threat his foes,
His eyes like glow-worms shine; when he doth fret
His snout digs sepulchres where'er he goes.
    Being moved, he strikes, whate'er is in his way,
    And whom he strikes his crooked tushes slay.

'His brawny sides, with hairy bristles armed
Are better proof than thy spear's point can enter.
His short thick neck cannot be easily harmed.
Being ireful, on the lion he will venture.
    The thorny brambles and embracing bushes,
    As fearful of him, part; through whom he rushes.

'Alas, he naught esteems that face of thine,
To which love's eyes pay tributary gazes,
Nor thy soft hands, sweet lips, and crystal eyne,
Whose full perfection all the world amazes;
    But having thee at vantage—wondrous dread!—
    Would root these beauties as he roots the mead.

'O, let him keep his loathsome cabin still.
Beauty hath naught to do with such foul fiends.
Come not within his danger by thy will.
They that thrive well take counsel of their friends.
　　When thou didst name the boar, not to dissemble,
　　I feared thy fortune, and my joints did tremble.

'Didst thou not mark my face? Was it not white?
Saw'st thou not signs of fear lurk in mine eye?
Grew I not faint, and fell I not downright?
Within my bosom, whereon thou dost lie,
　　My boding heart pants, beats, and takes no rest,
　　But like an earthquake shakes thee on my breast.

'For where love reigns, disturbing jealousy
Doth call himself affection's sentinel,
Gives false alarms, suggesteth mutiny,
And in a peaceful hour doth cry, "Kill, kill!",
　　Distemp'ring gentle love in his desire,
　　As air and water do abate the fire.

'This sour informer, this bate-breeding spy,
This canker that eats up love's tender spring,
This carry-tale, dissentious jealousy,
That sometime true news, sometime false doth bring,
　　Knocks at my heart, and whispers in mine ear
　　That if I love thee, I thy death should fear;

'And, more than so, presenteth to mine eye
The picture of an angry chafing boar,
Under whose sharp fangs on his back doth lie
An image like thyself, all stained with gore,
　　Whose blood upon the fresh flowers being shed
　　Doth make them droop with grief, and hang the head.

'What should I do, seeing thee so indeed,
That tremble at th'imagination?
The thought of it doth make my faint heart bleed,
And fear doth teach it divination.
    I prophesy thy death, my living sorrow,
    If thou encounter with the boar tomorrow.

'But if thou needs wilt hunt, be ruled by me:
Uncouple at the timorous flying hare,
Or at the fox which lives by subtlety,
Or at the roe which no encounter dare.
    Pursue these fearful creatures o'er the downs,
    And on thy well-breathed horse keep with thy hounds.

'And when thou hast on foot the purblind hare,
Mark the poor wretch, to overshoot his troubles,
How he outruns the wind, and with what care
He cranks and crosses with a thousand doubles.
    The many musits through the which he goes
    Are like a labyrinth to amaze his foes.

'Sometime he runs among a flock of sheep
To make the cunning hounds mistake their smell,
And sometime where earth-delving conies keep,
To stop the loud pursuers in their yell;
    And sometime sorteth with a herd of deer.
    Danger deviseth shifts; wit waits on fear.

'For there his smell with others being mingled,
The hot scent-snuffing hounds are driven to doubt,
Ceasing their clamorous cry till they have singled,
With much ado, the cold fault cleanly out.
    Then do they spend their mouths. Echo replies,
    As if another chase were in the skies.

'By this, poor Wat, far off upon a hill,
Stands on his hinder legs with list'ning ear,
To hearken if his foes pursue him still.
Anon their loud alarums he doth hear,
And now his grief may be comparèd well
To one sore sick that hears the passing-bell.

'Then shalt thou see the dew-bedabbled wretch
Turn, and return, indenting with the way.
Each envious brier his weary legs do scratch;
Each shadow makes him stop, each murmur stay;
    For misery is trodden on by many,
    And, being low, never relieved by any.

'Lie quietly, and hear a little more;
Nay, do not struggle, for thou shalt not rise.
To make thee hate the hunting of the boar
Unlike myself thou hear'st me moralize,
    Applying this to that, and so to so,
    For love can comment upon every woe.

'Where did I leave?' 'No matter where,' quoth he;
'Leave me, and then the story aptly ends.
The night is spent,' 'Why, what of that?' quoth she.
'I am,' quoth he, 'expected of my friends,
    And now 'tis dark, and going I shall fall.'
    'In night,' quoth she, 'desire sees best of all.

'But if thou fall, O, then imagine this:
The earth, in love with thee, thy footing trips,
And all is but to rob thee of a kiss.
Rich preys make true men thieves; so do thy lips
    Make modest Dian cloudy and forlorn
    Lest she should steal a kiss, and die forsworn.

'Now of this dark night I perceive the reason.
Cynthia, for shame, obscures her silver shine
Till forging nature be condemned of treason
For stealing moulds from heaven, that were divine,
    Wherein she framed thee, in high heaven's despite,
    To shame the sun by day and her by night.

'And therefore hath she bribed the destinies
To cross the curious workmanship of nature,
To mingle beauty with infirmities,
And pure perfection with impure defeature,
    Making it subject to the tyranny
    Of mad mischances and much misery;

'As burning fevers, agues pale and faint,
Life-poisoning pestilence and frenzies wood,
The marrow-eating sickness whose attaint
Disorder breeds by heating of the blood;
    Surfeits, impostumes, grief, and damned despair
    Swear nature's death for framing thee so fair.

'And not the least of all these maladies
But in one minute's fight brings beauty under.
Both favour, savour, hue, and qualities,
Whereat th'impartial gazer late did wonder,
    Are on the sudden wasted, thawed, and done,
    As mountain snow melts with the midday sun.

'Therefore, despite of fruitless chastity,
Love-lacking vestals and self-loving nuns,
That on the earth would breed a scarcity
And barren dearth of daughters and of sons,
    Be prodigal. The lamp that burns by night
    Dries up his oil to lend the world his light.

'What is thy body but a swallowing grave,
Seeming to bury that posterity
Which, by the rights of time, thou needs must have
If thou destroy them not in dark obscurity?
    If so, the world will hold thee in disdain,
    Sith in thy pride so fair a hope is slain.

'So in thyself thyself art made away,
A mischief worse than civil, home-bred strife,
Or theirs whose desperate hands themselves do slay,
Or butcher sire that reaves his son of life.
    Foul cank'ring rust the hidden treasure frets,
    But gold that's put to use more gold begets.'

'Nay, then,' quoth Adon, 'You will fall again
Into your idle over-handled theme.
The kiss I gave you is bestowed in vain,
And all in vain you strive against the stream;
    For, by this black-faced night, desire's foul nurse,
    Your treatise makes me like you worse and worse.

'If love have lent you twenty thousand tongues,
And every tongue more moving than your own,
Bewitching like the wanton mermaid's songs,
Yet from mine ear the tempting tune is blown;
    For know, my heart stands armèd in mine ear,
    And will not let a false sound enter there,

'Lest the deceiving harmony should run
Into the quiet closure of my breast,
And then my little heart were quite undone,
In his bedchamber to be barred of rest.
    No, lady, no. My heart longs not to groan,
    But soundly sleeps, while now it sleeps alone.

'What have you urged that I cannot reprove?
The path is smooth that leadeth on to danger.
I hate not love, but your device in love,
That lends embracements unto every stranger.
    You do it for increase—O strange excuse,
    When reason is the bawd to lust's abuse!

'Call it not love, for love to heaven is fled
Since sweating lust on earth usurped his name,
Under whose simple semblance he hath fed
Upon fresh beauty, blotting it with blame;
    Which the hot tyrant stains, and soon bereaves,
    As caterpillars do the tender leaves.

'Love comforteth, like sunshine after rain,
But lust's effect is tempest after sun.
Love's gentle spring doth always fresh remain;
Lust's winter comes ere summer half be done.
    Love surfeits not; lust like a glutton dies.
    Love is all truth, lust full of forgèd lies.

'More I could tell, but more I dare not say;
The text is old, the orator too green.
Therefore in sadness now I will away;
My face is full of shame, my heart of teen.
    Mine ears that to your wanton talk attended
    Do burn themselves for having so offended.'

With this he breaketh from the sweet embrace
Of those fair arms which bound him to her breast,
And homeward through the dark laund runs apace,
Leaves love upon her back, deeply distressed.
    Look how a bright star shooteth from the sky,
    So glides he in the night from Venus' eye,

Which after him she darts, as one on shore
Gazing upon a late-embarkèd friend
Till the wild waves will have him seen no more,
Whose ridges with the meeting clouds contend.
    So did the merciless and pitchy night
    Fold in the object that did feed her sight.

Whereat amazed, as one that unaware
Hath dropped a precious jewel in the flood,
Or stonished as night wand'rers often are,
Their light blown out in some mistrustful wood:
    Even so, confounded in the dark she lay,
    Having lost the fair discovery of her way.

And now she beats her heart, whereat it groans,
That all the neighbour caves, as seeming troubled,
Make verbal repetition of her moans;
Passion on passion deeply is redoubled.
    'Ay me,' she cries, and twenty times 'Woe, woe!'
    And twenty echoes twenty times cry so.

She, marking them, begins a wailing note,
And sings extemporally a woeful ditty,
How love makes young men thrall, and old men dote,
How love is wise in folly, foolish-witty.
    Her heavy anthem still concludes in woe,
    And still the choir of echoes answer so.

Her song was tedious, and outwore the night;
For lovers' hours are long, though seeming short.
If pleased themselves, others, they think, delight
In such-like circumstance, with such-like sport.
    Their copious stories oftentimes begun
    End without audience, and are never done.

For who hath she to spend the night withal
But idle sounds resembling parasites,
Like shrill-tongued tapsters answering every call,
Soothing the humour of fantastic wits?
　　She says ' 'Tis so'; they answer all ' 'Tis so,'
　　And would say after her, if she said 'No.'

Lo, here the gentle lark, weary of rest,
From his moist cabinet mounts up on high
And wakes the morning, from whose silver breast
The sun ariseth in his majesty,
　　Who doth the world so gloriously behold
　　That cedar tops and hills seem burnished gold.

Venus salutes him with this fair good-morrow:
'O thou clear god, and patron of all light,
From whom each lamp and shining star doth borrow
The beauteous influence that makes him bright:
　　There lives a son that sucked an earthly mother
　　May lend thee light, as thou dost lend to other.'

This said, she hasteth to a myrtle grove,
Musing the morning is so much o'erworn
And yet she hears no tidings of her love.
She hearkens for his hounds, and for his horn.
　　Anon she hears them chant it lustily,
　　And all in haste she coasteth to the cry.

And as she runs, the bushes in the way
Some catch her by the neck, some kiss her face,
Some twine about her thigh to make her stay.
She wildly breaketh from their strict embrace,
　　Like a milch doe whose swelling dugs do ache,
　　Hasting to feed her fawn hid in some brake.

By this she hears the hounds are at a bay,
Whereat she starts, like one that spies an adder
Wreathed up in fatal folds just in his way,
The fear whereof doth make him shake and shudder;
 Even so the timorous yelping of the hounds
 Appals her senses, and her spirit confounds.

For now she knows it is no gentle chase,
But the blunt boar, rough bear, or lion proud,
Because the cry remaineth in one place,
Where fearfully the dogs exclaim aloud.
 Finding their enemy to be so curst,
 They all strain court'sy who shall cope him first.

This dismal cry rings sadly in her ear,
Through which it enters to surprise her heart,
Who, overcome by doubt and bloodless fear,
With cold-pale weakness numbs each feeling part;
 Like soldiers, when their captain once doth yield,
 They basely fly, and dare not stay the field.

Thus stands she in a trembling ecstasy,
Till, cheering up her senses all dismayed,
She tells them 'tis a causeless fantasy
And childish error that they are afraid;
 Bids them leave quaking, bids them fear no more;
 And with that word she spied the hunted boar,

Whose frothy mouth, bepainted all with red,
Like milk and blood being mingled both together,
A second fear through all her sinews spread,
Which madly hurries her, she knows not whither.
 This way she runs, and now she will no further,
 But back retires to rate the boar for murder.

A thousand spleens bear her a thousand ways.
She treads the path that she untreads again.
Her more than haste is mated with delays,
Like the proceedings of a drunken brain,
 Full of respects, yet naught at all respecting;
 In hand with all things, naught at all effecting.

Here kennelled in a brake she finds a hound,
And asks the weary caitiff for his master;
And there another licking of his wound,
'Gainst venomed sores the only sovereign plaster.
 And here she meets another, sadly scowling,
 To whom she speaks; and he replies with howling.

When he hath ceased his ill-resounding noise,
Another flap-mouthed mourner, black and grim,
Against the welkin volleys out his voice.
Another, and another, answer him,
 Clapping their proud tails to the ground below,
 Shaking their scratched ears, bleeding as they go.

Look how the world's poor people are amazed
At apparitions, signs, and prodigies,
Whereon with fearful eyes they long have gazed,
Infusing them with dreadful prophecies:
 So she at these sad sighs draws up her breath,
 And, sighing it again, exclaims on death.

'Hard-favoured tyrant, ugly, meagre, lean,
Hateful divorce of love'—thus chides she death;
'Grim-grinning ghost, earth's worm: what dost thou mean
To stifle beauty, and to steal his breath
 Who, when he lived, his breath and beauty set
 Gloss on the rose, smell to the violet?

'If he be dead—O no, it cannot be,
Seeing his beauty, thou shouldst strike at it.
O yes, it may; thou hast no eyes to see,
But hatefully, at random dost thou hit.
    Thy mark is feeble age; but thy false dart
    Mistakes that aim, and cleaves an infant's heart.

'Hadst thou but bid beware, then he had spoke,
And, hearing him, thy power had lost his power.
The destinies will curse thee for this stroke.
They bid thee crop a weed; thou pluck'st a flower.
    Love's golden arrow at him should have fled,
    And not death's ebon dart to strike him dead.

'Dost thou drink tears, that thou provok'st such weeping?
What may a heavy groan advantage thee?
Why hast thou cast into eternal sleeping
Those eyes that taught all other eyes to see?
    Now nature cares not for thy mortal vigour,
    Since her best work is ruined with thy rigour.'

Here overcome, as one full of despair,
She vailed her eyelids, who like sluices stopped
The crystal tide that from her two cheeks fair
In the sweet channel of her bosom dropped.
    But through the flood-gates breaks the silver rain,
    And with his strong course opens them again.

O, how her eyes and tears did lend and borrow!
Her eye seen in the tears, tears in her eye,
Both crystals, where they viewed each other's sorrow:
Sorrow, that friendly sighs sought still to dry,
    But, like a stormy day, now wind, now rain,
    Sighs dry her cheeks, tears make them wet again.

Variable passions throng her constant woe,
As striving who should best become her grief.
All entertained, each passion labours so
That every present sorrow seemeth chief,
But none is best. Then join they all together,
Like many clouds consulting for foul weather.

By this, far off she hears some huntsman hollo;
A nurse's song ne'er pleased her babe so well.
The dire imagination she did follow
This sound of hope doth labour to expel;
    For now reviving joy bids her rejoice
    And flatters her it is Adonis' voice.

Whereat her tears began to turn their tide,
Being prisoned in her eye like pearls in glass;
Yet sometimes falls an orient drop beside,
Which her cheek melts, as scorning it should pass
    To wash the foul face of the sluttish ground,
    Who is but drunken when she seemeth drowned.

O hard-believing love—how strange it seems
Not to believe, and yet too credulous!
Thy weal and woe are both of them extremes.
Despair, and hope, make thee ridiculous.
    The one doth flatter thee in thoughts unlikely;
    In likely thoughts the other kills thee quickly.

Now she unweaves the web that she hath wrought.
Adonis lives, and death is not to blame.
It was not she that called him all to naught.
Now she adds honours to his hateful name.
    She clepes him king of graves, and grave for kings,
    Imperious supreme of all mortal things.

'No, no,' quoth she, 'sweet death, I did but jest.
Yet pardon me, I felt a kind of fear
Whenas I met the boar, that bloody beast,
Which knows no pity, but is still severe.
　　Then, gentle shadow—truth I must confess—
　　I railed on thee, fearing my love's decease.

' 'Tis not my fault; the boar provoked my tongue.
Be wreaked on him, invisible commander.
'Tis he, foul creature, that hath done thee wrong.
I did but act; he's author of thy slander.
　　Grief hath two tongues, and never woman yet
　　Could rule them both, without ten women's wit.'

Thus, hoping that Adonis is alive,
Her rash suspect she doth extenuate,
And that his beauty may the better thrive,
With death she humbly doth insinuate;
　　Tells him of trophies, statues, tombs; and stories
　　His victories, his triumphs, and his glories.

'O Jove,' quoth she, 'how much a fool was I
To be of such a weak and silly mind
To wail his death who lives, and must not die
Till mutual overthrow of mortal kind!
　　For he being dead, with him is beauty slain,
　　And beauty dead, black chaos comes again.

'Fie, fie, fond love, thou art so full of fear
As one with treasure laden, hemmed with thieves.
Trifles unwitnessèd with eye or ear,
Thy coward heart with false bethinking grieves.'
　　Even at this word she hears a merry horn,
　　Whereat she leaps, that was but late forlorn.

As falcons to the lure, away she flies.
The grass stoops not, she treads on it so light;
And in her haste unfortunately spies
The foul boar's conquest on her fair delight;
    Which seen, her eyes, as murdered with the view,
    Like stars ashamed of day, themselves withdrew.

Or as the snail, whose tender horns being hit
Shrinks backwards in his shelly cave with pain,
And there, all smothered up, in shade doth sit,
Long after fearing to creep forth again;
    So at his bloody view her eyes are fled
    Into the deep dark cabins of her head,

Where they resign their office and their light
To the disposing of her troubled brain,
Who bids them still consort with ugly night,
And never wound the heart with looks again,
    Who, like a king perplexèd in his throne,
    By their suggestion gives a deadly groan,

Whereat each tributary subject quakes,
As when the wind, imprisoned in the ground,
Struggling for passage, earth's foundation shakes,
Which with cold terror doth men's minds confound.
    This mutiny each part doth so surprise
    That from their dark beds once more leap her eyes,

And, being opened, threw unwilling light
Upon the wide wound that the boar had trenched
In his soft flank, whose wonted lily-white
With purple tears that his wound wept was drenched.
    No flower was nigh, no grass, herb, leaf, or weed,
    But stole his blood, and seemed with him to bleed.

This solemn sympathy poor Venus noteth.
Over one shoulder doth she hang her head.
Dumbly she passions, franticly she doteth.
She thinks he could not die, he is not dead.
　　Her voice is stopped, her joints forget to bow,
　　Her eyes are mad that they have wept till now.

Upon his hurt she looks so steadfastly
That her sight, dazzling, makes the wound seem three;
And then she reprehends her mangling eye,
That makes more gashes where no breach should be.
　　His face seems twain; each several limb is doubled;
　　For oft the eye mistakes, the brain being troubled.

'My tongue cannot express my grief for one,
And yet,' quoth she, 'behold two Adons dead!
My sighs are blown away, my salt tears gone,
Mine eyes are turned to fire, my heart to lead.
　　Heavy heart's lead, melt at mine eyes' red fire!
　　So shall I die by drops of hot desire.

'Alas, poor world, what treasure hast thou lost,
What face remains alive that's worth the viewing?
Whose tongue is music now? What canst thou boast
Of things long since, or anything ensuing?
　　The flowers are sweet, their colours fresh and trim;
　　But true sweet beauty lived and died with him.

'Bonnet nor veil henceforth no creature wear:
Nor sun nor wind will ever strive to kiss you.
Having no fair to lose, you need not fear.
The sun doth scorn you, and the wind doth hiss you.
　　But when Adonis lived, sun and sharp air
　　Lurked like two thieves to rob him of his fair;

'And therefore would he put his bonnet on,
Under whose brim the gaudy sun would peep.
The wind would blow it off, and, being gone,
Play with his locks; then would Adonis weep,
    And straight, in pity of his tender years,
    They both would strive who first should dry his tears.

'To see his face the lion walked along
Behind some hedge, because he would not fear him.
To recreate himself when he hath sung,
The tiger would be tame, and gently hear him.
    If he had spoke, the wolf would leave his prey,
    And never fright the silly lamb that day.

'When he beheld his shadow in the brook,
The fishes spread on it their golden gills.
When he was by, the birds such pleasure took
That some would sing, some other in their bills
    Would bring him mulberries and ripe-red cherries.
    He fed them with his sight, they him with berries.

'But this foul, grim, and urchin-spouted boar,
Whose downward eye still looketh for a grave,
Ne'er saw the beauteous livery that he wore:
Witness the entertainment that he gave.
    If he did see his face, why then, I know
    He thought to kiss him, and hath killed him so.

' 'Tis true, 'tis true; thus was Adonis slain;
He ran upon the boar with his sharp spear,
Who did not whet his teeth at him again,
But by a kiss thought to persuade him there,
    And, nuzzling in his flank, the loving swine
    Sheathed unaware the tusk in his soft groin.

'Had I been toothed like him, I must confess
With kissing him I should have killed him first;
But he is dead, and never did he bless
My youth with his, the more am I accursd.'
    With this she falleth in the place she stood,
    And stains her face with his congealèd blood.

Sho looks upon his lips, and they are pale.
She takes him by the hand, and that is cold.
She whispers in his ears a heavy tale,
As if they heard the woeful words she told.
    She lifts the coffer-lids that close his eyes,
    Where lo, two lamps burnt out in darkness lies;

Two glasses, where herself herself beheld
A thousand times, and now no more reflect,
Their virtue lost, wherein they late excelled,
And every beauty robbed of his effect.
    'Wonder of time,' quoth she, 'this is my spite,
    That, you being dead, the day should yet be light.

'Since thou art dead, lo, here I prophesy
Sorrow on love hereafter shall attend.
It shall be waited on with jealousy,
Find sweet beginning, but unsavoury end;
    Ne'er settled equally, but high or low,
    That all love's pleasure shall not match his woe.

'It shall be fickle, false, and full of fraud,
Bud, and be blasted, in a breathing-while:
The bottom poison, and the top o'erstrawed
With sweets that shall the truest sight beguile.
    The strongest body shall it make most weak,
    Strike the wise dumb, and teach the fool to speak.

'It shall be sparing, and too full of riot,
Teaching decrepit age to tread the measures.
The staring ruffian shall it keep in quiet,
Pluck down the rich, enrich the poor with treasures;
    It shall be raging-mad, and silly-mild;
    Make the young old, the old become a child.

'It shall suspect where is no cause of fear;
It shall not fear where it should most mistrust.
It shall be merciful, and too severe,
And most deceiving when it seems most just.
    Perverse it shall be where it shows most toward,
    Put fear to valour, courage to the coward.

'It shall be cause of war and dire events,
And set dissension 'twixt the son and sire;
Subject and servile to all discontents,
As dry combustious matter is to fire.
    Sith in his prime death doth my love destroy,
    They that love best their loves shall not enjoy.'

By this, the boy that by her side lay killed
Was melted like a vapour from her sight,
And in his blood that on the ground lay spilled
A purple flower sprung up, chequered with white,
    Resembling well his pale cheeks, and the blood
    Which in round drops upon their whiteness stood.

She bows her head the new-sprung flower to smell,
Comparing it to her Adonis' breath,
And says within her bosom it shall dwell,
Since he himself is reft from her by death.
    She drops the stalk, and in the breach appears
    Green-dropping sap, which she compares to tears.

'Poor flower,' quoth she, 'this was thy father's guise—
Sweet issue of a more sweet-smelling sire—
For every little grief to wet his eyes.
To grow unto himself was his desire,
    And so 'tis thine; but know it is as good
    To wither in my breast as in his blood.

'Here was thy father's bed, here in my breast.
Thou art the next of blood, and 'tis thy right.
Lo, in this hollow cradle take thy rest;
My throbbing heart shall rock thee day and night.
    There shall not be one minute in an hour
    Wherein I will not kiss my sweet love's flower.'

Thus, weary of the world, away she hies,
And yokes her silver doves, by whose swift aid
Their mistress, mounted, through the empty skies
In her light chariot quickly is conveyed,
    Holding their course to Paphos, where their queen
    Means to immure herself, and not be seen.

# THE PHOENIX
# AND THE TURTLE

Let the bird of loudest lay
On the sole Arabian tree
Herald sad and trumpet be,
To whose sound chaste wings obey.

But thou shrieking harbinger,
Foul precurrer of the fiend,
Augur of the fever's end—
To this troupe come thou not near.

From this session interdict
Every fowl of tyrant wing
Save the eagle, feathered king.
Keep the obsequy so strict.

Let the priest in surplice white
That defunctive music can,
Be the death-divining swan,
Lest the requiem lack his right.

And thou treble-dated crow,
That thy sable gender mak'st
With the breath thou giv'st and tak'st,
'Mongst our mourners shalt thou go.

Here the anthem doth commence:
Love and constancy is dead,
Phoenix and the turtle fled
In a mutual flame from hence.

So they loved as love in twain
Had the essence but in one,
Two distincts, division none.
Number there in love was slain.

Hearts remote yet not asunder,
Distance and no space was seen
'Twixt the turtle and his queen.
But in them it were a wonder.

So between them love did shine
That the turtle saw his right
Flaming in the phoenix' sight.
Either was the other's mine.

Property was thus appalled
That the self was not the same.
Single nature's double name
Neither two nor one was called.

Reason, in itself confounded,
Saw division grow together
To themselves, yet either neither,
Simple were so well compounded

That it cried 'How true a twain
Seemeth this concordant one!
Love hath reason, reason none,
If what parts can so remain.'

Whereupon it made this threne
To the phoenix and the dove,
Co-supremes and stars of love,
As chorus to their tragic scene.

*Threnos*

Beauty, truth, and rarity,
Grace in all simplicity,
Here enclosed in cinders lie.

Death is now the phoenix' nest,
And the turtle's loyal breast
To eternity doth rest.

Leaving no posterity
'Twas not their infirmity,
It was married chastity.

Truth may seem but cannot be,
Beauty brag, but 'tis not she.
Truth and beauty buried be.

To this urn let those repair
That are either true or fair.
For these dead birds sigh a prayer.

# APPENDIX

## The Portrait of Mr. W. H.
### Oscar Wilde

1

I had been dining with Erskine in his pretty little house in Birdcage Walk, and we were sitting in the library over our coffee and cigarettes, when the question of literary forgeries happened to turn up in conversation. I cannot at present remember how it was that we struck upon this somewhat curious topic, as it was at that time, but I know that we had a long discussion about Macpherson, Ireland, and Chatterton, and that with regard to the last I insisted that his so-called forgeries were merely the result of an artistic desire for perfect representation; that we had no right to quarrel with an artist for the conditions under which he chooses to present his work; and that all Art being to a certain degree a mode of acting, an attempt to realise one's own personality on some imaginative plane out of reach of the trammelling accidents and limitations of real life, to censure an artist for a forgery was to confuse an ethical with an æsthetical problem.

Erskine, who was a good deal older than I was, and had been listening to me with the amused deference of a man of forty, suddenly put his hand upon my shoulder and said to me, "What would you say about a young man who had a strange theory about a certain work of art, believed in his theory, and committed a forgery in order to prove it?"

"Ah! that is quite a different matter," I answered.

Erskine remained silent for a few moments, looking at the thin grey threads of smoke that were rising from his cigarette. "Yes," he said, after a pause, "quite different."

There was something in the tone of his voice, a slight touch of bitterness perhaps, that excited my curiosity. "Did you ever know anybody who did that?" I cried.

"Yes," he answered, throwing his cigarette into the fire—"a great friend of mine, Cyril Graham. He was very fascinating, and very foolish, and very heartless. However, he left me the only legacy I ever received in my life."

"What was that?" I exclaimed laughing. Erskine rose from his seat, and going over to a tall inlaid cabinet that stood between the two windows, unlocked it, and came back to where I was sitting, carrying

a small panel picture set in an old and somewhat tarnished Elizabe-
than frame.

It was a full-length portrait of a young man in late sixteenth-cen-
tury costume, standing by a table, with his right hand resting on an
open book. He seemed about seventeen years of age, and was of quite
extraordinary personal beauty, though evidently somewhat effeminate.
Indeed, had it not been for the dress and the closely cropped hair, one
would have said that the face, with its dreamy wistful eyes and its
delicate scarlet lips, was the face of a girl. In manner, and especially in
the treatment of the hands, the picture reminded one of François
Clouet's later work. The black velvet doublet with its fantastically
gilded points, and the peacock-blue background against which it showed
up so pleasantly, and from which it gained such luminous value of
colour, were quite in Clouet's style; and the two masks of Tragedy and
Comedy that hung somewhat formally from the marble pedestal had
that hard severity of touch—so different from the facile grace of the
Italians—which even at the Court of France the great Flemish master
never completely lost, and which in itself has always been a character-
istic of the northern temper.

"It is a charming thing," I cried, "but who is this wonderful young
man whose beauty Art has so happily preserved for us?"

"This is the portrait of Mr. W. H.," said Erskine, with a sad smile.
It might have been a chance effect of light, but it seemed to me that
his eyes were swimming with tears.

"Mr. W. H.!" I repeated; "who was Mr. W. H.?"

"Don't you remember?" he answered; "look at the book on which
his hand is resting."

"I see there is some writing there, but I cannot make it out," I
replied.

"Take this magnifying-glass and try," said Erskine, with the same
sad smile still playing about his mouth.

I took the glass, and moving the lamp a little nearer, I began to
spell out the crabbed sixteenth-century handwriting. "To The Onlie
Begetter Of These Insuing Sonnets." . . . "Good heavens!" I cried, "is
this Shakespeare's Mr. W. H.?"

"Cyril Graham used to say so," muttered Erskine.

"But it is not a bit like Lord Pembroke," I rejoined. "I know the
Wilton portraits very well. I was staying near there a few weeks ago."

"Do you really believe then that the Sonnets are addressed to Lord
Pembroke?" he asked.

"I am sure of it," I answered. "Pembroke, Shakespeare, and Mrs. Mary Fitton are the three personages of the Sonnets; there is no doubt at all about it."

"Well, I agree with you," said Erskine, "but I did not always think so. I used to believe—well, I suppose I used to believe in Cyril Graham and his theory."

"And what was that?" I asked, looking at the wonderful portrait, which had already begun to have a strange fascination for me.

"It is a long story," said Erskine, taking the picture away from me—rather abruptly I thought at the time—"a very long story; but if you care to hear it, I will tell it to you."

"I love theories about the Sonnets," I cried; "but I don't think I am likely to be converted to any new idea. The matter has ceased to be a mystery to any one. Indeed, I wonder that it ever was a mystery."

"As I don't believe in the theory, I am not likely to convert you to it," said Erskine, laughing; "but it may interest you."

"Tell it to me, of course," I answered. "If it is half as delightful as the picture, I shall be more than satisfied."

"Well," said Erskine, lighting a cigarette, "I must begin by telling you about Cyril Graham himself. He and I were at the same house at Eton. I was a year or two older than he was, but we were immense friends, and did all our work and all our play together. There was, of course, a good deal more play than work, but I cannot say that I am sorry for that. It is always an advantage not to have received a sound commercial education, and what I learned in the playing fields at Eton has been quite as useful to me as anything I was taught at Cambridge. I should tell you that Cyril's father and mother were both dead. They had been drowned in a horrible yachting accident off the Isle of Wight. His father had been in the Diplomatic Service, and had married a daughter, the only daughter, in fact, of old Lord Crediton, who became Cyril's guardian after the death of his parents. I don't think that Lord Crediton cared very much for Cyril. He had never really forgiven his daughter for marrying a man who had not a title. He was an extraordinary old aristocrat, who swore like a costermonger, and had the manners of a farmer. I remember seeing him once on Speech-day. He growled at me, gave me a sovereign, and told me not to grow up 'a damned Radical' like my father. Cyril had very little affection for him, and was only too glad to spend most of his holidays with us in Scotland. They never really got on together at all. Cyril thought him a bear, and he thought Cyril effeminate. He was effeminate, I suppose, in some things, though he was a capital rider and a capital fencer. In fact he got the foils before he left Eton. But he was very languid in his manner, and not a little vain of his good looks, and had a strong objection to football, which he used to say was a game only suitable for the sons of the middle classes. The two things that really gave him pleasure were poetry and acting. At Eton he was always dressing up and reciting Shakespeare, and when we went up to Trinity he became a member of the A.D.C. his first term. I remember I was always very jealous of his acting. I was absurdly devoted to him; I suppose because we were so different in some things. I was a rather awkward, weakly lad, with huge feet, and horribly freckled. Freckles run in Scotch families just as gout does in English families. Cyril used to say that of the two he preferred the gout; but he always set an absurdly high value on personal appearance, and once read a paper before our Debating Society to prove that it was better to be good-looking than to be good. He certainly was wonderfully handsome. People who did not like him, philistines and college tutors, and young men reading for the Church, used to say that he was merely pretty; but there was a great deal more in his face than mere prettiness. I think he was the most splendid creature I ever saw, and nothing could ex-ceed the grace of his movements, the charm of his manner. He fasci-nated everybody who was worth fascinating, and a great many people who were not. He was often wilful and petulant, and I used to think him dreadfully insincere. It was due, I think, chiefly to his inordinate desire to please. Poor Cyril! I told him once that he was contented with very cheap triumphs, but he only tossed his head, and smiled. He was horribly spoiled. All charming people, I fancy, are spoiled. It is the secret of their attraction.

"However, I must tell you about Cyril's acting. You know that no women are allowed to play at the A.D.C. At least they were not in my time. I don't know how it is now. Well, of course Cyril was always cast for the girls' parts, and when *As You Like It* was produced he played Rosalind. It was a marvellous performance. You will laugh at me, bit I assure you that Cyril Graham was the only perfect Rosalind I have ever seen. It would be impossible to describe to you the beauty, the delicacy, the refinement of the whole thing. It made an immense sensation, and the horrid little theatre as it was then, was crowded every night. Even now when I read the play I can't help thinking of Cyril; the part might have been written for him, he played it with such extraordinary grace and distinction. The next term he took his degree, and came to London to read for the Diplomatic. But he never did any work. He spent his days in reading Shakespeare's Sonnets, and his evenings at the theatre. He was, of course, wild to go on the stage. It was all that Lord Crediton and I could do to prevent him. Perhaps, if he had gone on the stage he would be alive now. It is always a silly thing to give advice, but to give good advice is absolutely fatal. I hope you will never fall into that error. If you do, you will be sorry for it.

"Well, to come to the real point of the story, one afternoon I got a letter from Cyril asking me to come round to his rooms that evening. He had charming chambers in Piccadilly overlooking the Green Park, and as I used to go to see him every day, I was rather surprised at his taking the trouble to write. Of course I went, and when I arrived I found him in a state of great excitement. He told me that he had at last discovered the true secret of Shakespeare's Sonnets; that all the scholars and critics had been entirely on the wrong track; and that he was the first who, working purely by internal evidence, had found out who Mr. W. H. really was. He was perfectly wild with delight, and for a long time would not tell me his theory. Finally, he produced a bundle of notes, took his copy of the Sonnets off the mantelpiece, and sat down and gave me a long lecture on the whole subject.

"He began by pointing out that the young man to whom Shakespeare addressed these strangely passionate poems must have been somebody who was a really vital factor in the development of his dramatic art, and that this could not be said of either Lord Pembroke or Lord Southampton. Indeed, whoever he was, he could not have been anybody of high birth, as was shown very clearly by the Sonnet 25, in which Shakespeare contrasts himself with men who are 'great princes' favourites'; says quite frankly—

> Let those who are in favour with their stars
> Of public honour and proud titles boast,
> Whilst I, whom fortune of such triumph bars,
> Unlooked-for joy in that I honor most;

and ends the sonnet by congratulating himself on the mean state of him he so adored:

> Then happy I, that loved and am beloved
> Where I may not remove nor be removed.

This sonnet Cyril declared would be quite unintelligible if we fancied that it was addressed to either the Earl of Pembroke or the Earl of Southhampton, both of whom were men of the highest position in England and fully entitled to be called 'great princes'; and he in corroboration of his view read me Sonnets 124 and 125, in which Shakespeare tells us that his love is not 'the child of state,' that it 'suffers not in smiling pomp,' but is 'builded far from accident.' I listened with a good deal of interest, for I don't think the point had ever been made before; but what followed was still more curious, and seemed to me at the time to dispose entirely of Pembroke's claim. We know from Meres that the Sonnets had been written before 1598, and Sonnet 104 informs us that Shakespeare's friendship for Mr. W. H. had been already in existence for three years. Now Lord Pembroke, who was born in 1580, did not come to London till he was eighteen years of age, that is to say till 1598, and Shakespeare's acquaintance with Mr. W. H. must have begun in 1594, or at the latest in 1595. Shakespeare, accordingly, could not have known Lord Pembroke till after the Sonnets had been written.

"Cyril pointed out also that Pembroke's father did not die till 1601; whereas it was evident from the line,

You had a father, let your son say so,

that the father of Mr. W. H. was dead in 1598; and laid great stress on the evidence afforded by the Wilton portraits which represent Lord Pembroke as a swarthy dark-haired man, while Mr. W. H. was one whose hair was like spun gold, and whose face was the meeting-place for the 'lily's white' and the 'deep vermilion in the rose'; being himself 'fair,' and 'red,' and 'white and red,' and of beautiful aspect. Besides it was absurd to imagine that any publisher of the time, and the preface is from the publisher's hand, would have dreamed of addressing William Herbert, Earl of Pembroke, as Mr. W. H.; the case of Lord Buckhurst being spoken of as Mr. Sackville being not really a parallel instance, as Lord Buckhurst, the first of that title, was plain Mr. Sackville when he contributed to the *Mirror for Magistrates*, while Pembroke, during his father's lifetime, was always known as Lord Herbert. So far for Lord Pembroke, whose supposed claims Cyril easily demolished while I sat by in wonder. With Lord Southampton Cyril had even less difficulty. Southampton became at a very early age the lover of Elizabeth Vernon, so he needed no entreaties to marry; he was not beautiful; he did not resemble his mother, as Mr. W. H. did—

> Thou art thy mother's glass, and she in thee
> Calls back the lovely April of her prime;

and, above all, his Christian name was Henry, whereas the punning sonnets (135 and 143) show that the Christian name of Shakespeare's friend was the same as his own—*Will*.

"As for the other suggestions of unfortunate commentators, that Mr. W. H. is a misprint for Mr. W. S., meaning Mr. William Shakespeare; that 'Mr. W. H. all' should read 'Mr. W. Hall'; that Mr. W. H. is Mr. William Hathaway; that Mr. W. H. stands for Mr. Henry Willobie, the young Oxford poet, with the initials of his name reversed; and that a full stop should be placed after 'wisheth,' making Mr. W. H. the writer and not the subject of the dedication—Cyril got rid of them in a very short time; and it is not worth while to mention his reasons, though I remember he sent me off into a fit of laughter by reading to me, I am glad to say not in the original, some extracts from a German commentator called Barnstorff, who insisted that Mr. W. H. was no less a person than 'Mr. William Himself.' Nor would he allow for a moment that the Sonnets are mere satires on the work of Drayton and John Davies of Hereford. To him, as indeed to me, they were poems of serious and tragic import, wrung out of the bitterness of Shakespeare's heart, and made sweet by the honey of his lips. Still less would he admit that they were merely a philosophical allegory, and that in them Shakespeare is addressing his Ideal Self, or Ideal Manhood, or the Spirit of Beauty, or the Reason, or the Divine Logos, or the Catholic Church. He felt, as indeed I think we all must feel, that the Sonnets are addressed to an individual—to a particular young man whose personality for some reason seems to have filled the soul of Shakespeare with terrible joy and no less terrible despair.

"Having in this manner cleared the way, as it were, Cyril asked me to dismiss from my mind any preconceived ideas I might have formed on the subject, and to give a fair and unbiased hearing to his own theory. The problem he pointed out was this: Who was that young man of Shakespeare's day who, without being of noble birth or even of noble nature, was addressed by him in terms of such passionate adoration that we can but wonder at the strange worship, and are almost afraid to turn the key that unlocks the mystery of the poet's heart? Who was he whose physical beauty was such that it became the very corner-stone of Shakespeare's art; the very source of Shakespeare's inspiration; the very incarnation of Shakespeare's dreams? To look

upon him as simply the object of certain love-poems was to miss the
whole meaning of the poems: for the art of which Shakespeare talks
in the Sonnets is not the art of the Sonnets themselves, which indeed
were to him but slight and secret things—it is the art of the dramatist
to which he is always alluding; and he to whom Shakespeare said—

> Thou art all my art, and dost advance
> As high as learning my rude ignorance,

he to whom he promised immortality,

> Where breath most breathes, even in the mouths of men,

he who was to him the tenth 'muse' and

> Ten times more in worth
> Than those old nine which rhymers invoke,

was surely none other than the boy-actor for whom he created Viola
and Imogen, Juliet and Rosalind, Portia and Desdemona, and
Cleopatra herself.

"The boy-actor of Shakespeare's plays?" I cried.

"Yes," said Erskine. "This was Cyril Graham's theory, evolved as
you see purely from the Sonnets themselves, and depending for its
acceptance not so much on demonstrable proof or formal evidence,
but on a kind of spiritual and artistic sense, by which alone he claimed
could the true meaning of the poems be discerned.  I remember his
reading to me that fine sonnet—

> How can my Muse want subject to invent,
> While thou dost breathe, that pour'st into my verse
> Thine own sweet argument, too excellent
> For every vulgar paper to rehearse
> O give thyself the thanks, if aught in me
> Worthy perusal stand against thy sight;
> For who's so dumb that cannot write to thee,
> When thou thyself dost give invention light?

—and pointing out how completely it corroborated his view; and in-
deed he went through all the Sonnets carefully, and showed, or fan-
cied that he showed, that, according to his new explanation of their
meaning, things that had seemed obscure, or evil, or exaggerated, be-
came clear and rational, and of high artistic import, illustrating

Shakespeare's conception of the true relations between the art of the
actor and the art of the dramatist.

"It is of course evident that there must have been in Shakespeare's
company some wonderful boy-actor of great beauty, to whom he in-
trusted the presentation of his noble heroines; for Shakespeare was a
practical theatrical manager as well as an imaginative poet, and Cyril
Graham had actually discovered the boy-actor's name. He was Will,
or as he preferred to call him, Willie Hughes. The Christian name he
found of course in the punning sonnets, 135 and 143; the surname
was, according to him, hidden in the seventh line of Sonnet 20, where
Mr. W. H. is described as—

> A man in hew, all *Hews* in his controwling.

"In the original edition of the Sonnets 'Hews' is printed with a
capital letter and in italics, and this, he claimed, showed clearly that a
play on words was intended, his view receiving a good deal of corrobo-
ration from those sonnets in which curious puns are made on the
words 'use' and 'usury,' and from such lines as—

> Thou art as fair in knowledge as in hew.

Of course I was converted at once, and Willie Hughes became to
me as real a person as Shakespeare. The only objection I made to the
theory was that the name of Willie Hughes does not occur in the list
of the actors of Shakespeare's company as it is printed in the first
folio. Cyril, however, pointed out that the absence of Willie Hughes'
name from this list really corroborated the theory, as it was evident
from Sonnet 86, that he had abandoned Shakespeare's company to
play at a rival theatre, probably in some of Chapman's plays. It was in
reference to this that in the great sonnet on Chapman Shakespeare
said to Willie Hughes—

> But when your countenance filed up his line,
> Then lacked I matter; that enfeebled mine—

the expression 'when your countenance filled up his line' referring
clearly to the beauty of the young actor giving life and reality and
added charm to Chapman's verse, the same idea being also put for-
ward in Sonnet 79:

> Whilst I alone did call upon thy aid,
> My verse alone had all thy gentle grace,
> But now my gracious numbers are decayed,
> And my sick Muse does give another place;

and in the immediately preceding sonnet, where Shakespeare says,

> Every alien pen has got my *use*
> And under thee their poesy disperse,

the play upon words (use = Hughes) being of course obvious, and the phrase 'under thee their poesy disperse,' meaning 'by your assistance as an actor bring their plays before the people.'

"It was a wonderful evening, and we sat up almost till dawn reading and re-reading the Sonnets. After some time, however, I began to see that before the theory could be placed before the world in a really perfected form, it was necessary to get some independent evidence about the existence of this young actor, Willie Hughes. If this could be once established, there could be no possible doubt about his identity with Mr. W. H.; but otherwise the theory would fall to the ground. I put this forward very strongly to Cyril, who was a good deal annoyed at what he called my philistine tone of mind, and indeed was rather bitter upon the subject. However, I made him promise that in his own interest he would not publish his discovery till he had put the whole matter beyond the reach of doubt; and for weeks and weeks we searched the registers of City Churches, the Alleyn MSS. at Dulwich, the Record Office, the books of the Lord Chamberlain—everything, in fact, that we thought might contain some allusion to Willie Hughes. We discovered nothing, of course, and each day the existence of Willie Hughes seemed to me to become more problematical. Cyril was in a dreadful state, and used to go over the whole question again and again, entreating me to believe; but I saw the one flaw in the theory, and I refused to be convinced till the actual existence of Willie Hughes, a boy-actor of Elizabethan stage, had been placed beyond the reach of doubt or cavil.

"One day Cyril left town to stay with his grandfather, I thought at the time, but I afterwards heard from Lord Crediton that this was not the case; and about a fortnight afterwards I received a telegram from him, handed in at Warwick, asking me to be sure to come and dine with him in his chambers, that evening at eight o'clock. When I arrived, he said to me, 'The only apostle who did not deserve proof was

St. Thomas, and St. Thomas was the only apostle who got it.' I asked him what he meant. He answered that he had not merely been able to establish the existence in the sixteenth century of a boy-actor of the name of Willie Hughes, but to prove by the most conclusive evidence that he was the Mr. W. H. of the Sonnets. He would not tell me anything more at the time; but after dinner he solemnly produced the picture I showed you, and told me that he had discovered it by the merest chance nailed to the side of an old chest that he had bought at a farmhouse in Warwickshire. The chest itself, which was a very fine example of Elizabethan work, and thoroughly authentic, he had, of course, brought with him, and in the centre of the front panel the initials W. H. were undoubtedly carved. It was this monogram that had attracted his attention, and he told me that it was not till he had had the chest in his possession for several days that he had thought of making any careful examination of the inside. One morning, however, he saw that the right-hand side of the chest was much thicker than the other, and looking more closely, he discovered that a framed panel picture was clamped against it. On taking it out, he found it was the picture that is now lying on the sofa. It was very dirty, and covered with mould; but he managed to clean it, and, to his great joy, saw that he had fallen by mere chance on the one thing for which he had been looking. Here was an authentic portrait of Mr. W. H., with his hand resting on the dedicatory page of the Sonnets, and on the corner of the picture could be faintly seen the name of the young man himself written in black uncial letters on the faded *bleu de paon* ground, 'Master Will Hews.'

"Well, what was I to say? It is quite clear from Sonnet 47 that Shakespeare had a portrait of M. W. H. in his possession, and it seemed to me more than probable that here we had the very 'painted banquet' on which he invited his eye to feast; the actual picture that awoke his heart 'to heart's and eye's delight.' It never occurred to me for a moment that Cyril Graham was playing a trick on me, or that he was trying to prove his theory by means of a forgery."

"But is it a forgery?" I asked.

"Of course it is," said Erskine. "It is a very good forgery; but it is a forgery none the less. I thought at the time that Cyril was rather calm about the whole matter; but I remember he kept telling me that he himself required no proof of the kind, and that he thought the theory complete without it. I laughed at him, and told him that without it the entire theory would fall to the ground, and I warmly congratulated him on the marvellous discovery. We then arranged that the picture should be etched or facsimiled, and placed as the frontispiece to Cyril's edition of the Sonnets; and for three months we did nothing but go over each poem line by line, till we had settled every difficulty of text or meaning. One unlucky day I was in a print-shop in Holborn, when I saw upon the counter some extremely beautiful drawings in silver-point. I was so attracted by them that I bought them; and the proprietor of the place, a man called Rawlings, told me that they were done by a young painter of the name of Edward Merton, who was very clever, but as poor as a church mouse. I went to see Merton some days afterwards, having got his address from the print-seller, and found a pale, interesting young man, with a rather common-looking wife—his model, as I subsequently learned. I told him how much I admired his drawings, at which he seemed very pleased, and I asked him if he would show me some of his other work. As we were looking over a portfolio, full of really lovely things—for Merton had a most delicate and delightful touch—I suddenly caught sight of a drawing of the picture of Mr. W. H. There was no doubt whatever about it. It was almost a facsimile—the only difference being that the two masks of Tragedy and Comedy were not suspended from the marble table as they are in the picture but were lying on the floor at the young man's feet. 'Where on earth did you get that?' I said. He grew rather confused, and said—'Oh, that is nothing. I did not know it was in this portfolio. It is not a thing of any value.' 'It is what you did for Mr. Cyril Graham,' exclaimed his wife; 'and if this gentleman wishes to buy it, let him have it.' 'For Mr. Cyril Graham?' I repeated. 'Did you paint the picture of Mr. W. H.?' 'I don't understand what you mean,' he answered, growing very red. Well, the whole thing was quite dreadful. The wife let it all out. I gave her five pounds when I was going away. I can't bear to think of it, now; but of course I was furious. I went off at once to Cyril's chambers, waited there for three hours before he came in, with that horrid lie staring me in the face, and told him I had discovered his forgery. He grew very pale and said—'I did it purely for your sake. You would not be convinced in any other way. It does not affect the truth of the theory.' 'The truth of the theory!' I exclaimed; 'the less we talk about that the better. You never even believed in it yourself. If you had, you would not have committed a forgery to prove it.' High words passed between us; we had a fearful quarrel. I daresay I was unjust, and the next morning he was dead."

"Dead!" I cried.

"Yes; he shot himself with a revolver. By the time I arrived—his servant had sent for me at once—the police were already there. He had left a letter for me, evidently written in the greatest agitation and distress of mind."

"What was in it?" I asked.

"Oh, that he believed absolutely in Willie Hughes; that the forgery of the picture had been done simply as a concession to me, and did not in the slightest degree invalidate the truth of the theory; and that in order to show me how firm and flawless his faith in the whole thing was, he was going to offer his life as a sacrifice to the secret of the Sonnets. It was a foolish, mad letter. I remember he ended by saying that he intrusted to me the Willie Hughes theory, and that it was for me to present it to the world, and to unlock the secret of Shakespeare's heart."

"It is a most tragic story," I cried, "but why have you not carried out his wishes?"

Erskine shrugged his shoulders. "Because it is a perfectly unsound theory from beginning to end," he answered.

"My dear Erskine," I exclaimed, getting up from my seat, "you are entirely wrong about the whole matter. It is the only perfect key to Shakespeare's Sonnets that has ever been made. It is complete in every detail. I believe in Willie Hughes."

"Don't say that," said Erskine gravely; "I believe there is something fatal about the idea, and intellectually there its nothing to be said for it. I have gone into the whole matter, and I assure you the theory is entirely fallacious. It is plausible up to a certain point. Then it stops. For heaven's sake, my dear boy, don't take up the subject of Willie Hughes. You will break your heart over it."

"Erskine," I answered, "it is your duty to give this theory to the world. If you will not do it, I will. By keeping it back you wrong the memory of Cyril Graham, the youngest and the most splendid of all the martyrs of literature. I entreat you to do him this bare act of justice. He died for this thing—don't let his death be in vain."

Erskine looked at me in amazement. "You are carried away by the sentiment of the whole story," he said. "You forget that a thing is not necessarily true because a man dies for it. I was devoted to Cyril Graham. His death was a horrible blow to me. I did not recover from it for years. I don't think I have ever recovered from it. But Willie Hughes! There is nothing in the idea of Willie Hughes. No such person ever existed. As for bringing the matter before the world—the world thinks that Cyril Graham shot himself by accident. The only proof of his suicide was contained in the letter to me, and of this letter the public never heard anything. To the present day Lord Crediton is under the impression that the whole thing was accidental."

"Cyril Graham sacrificed his life to a great idea," I answered; "and if you will not tell of his martyrdom, tell at least of his faith."

"His faith," said Erskine, "was fixed in a thing that was false, in a thing that was unsound, in a thing that no Shakespearian scholar would accept for a moment. The theory would be laughed at. Don't make a fool of yourself, and don't follow a trail that leads nowhere. You start by assuming the existence of the very person whose existence is the thing to be proved. Besides, everybody knows that the Sonnets were addressed to Lord Pembroke. The matter is settled once for all."

"The matter is not settled!" I exclaimed. "I will take up the theory where Cyril Graham left it, and I will prove to the world that he was right."

"Silly boy!" said Erskine. "Go home, it is after three, and don't think about Willie Hughes any more. I am sorry I told you anything about it, and very sorry indeed that I should have converted you to a thing in which I don't believe."

"You have given me the key to the greatest mystery of modern literature," I answered; "and I will not rest till I have made you recognise, till I have made everybody recognise, that Cyril Graham was the most subtle Shakespearian critic of our day."

I was about to leave the room when Erskine called me back. "My dear fellow," he said, "let me advise you not to waste your time over the Sonnets. I am quite serious. After all, what do they tell us about Shakespeare? Simply that he was the slave of beauty."

"Well, that is the condition of being an artist!" I replied.

There was a strange silence for a few moments. Then Erskine got up, and looking at me with half-closed eyes, said, "Ah! how you remind me of Cyril! He used to say just that sort of thing to me." He tried to smile, but there was a note of poignant pathos in his voice that I remember to the present day, as one remembers the tone of a particular violin that has charmed one, the touch of a particular woman's hand. The great events of life often leave one unmoved; they pass out of consciousness, and, when one thinks of them, become unreal. Even the scarlet flowers of passion seem to grow in the same meadow as the poppies of oblivion. We regret the burden of their memory, and have anodynes against them. But the little things, the things of no moment, remain with us. In some tiny ivory cell the brain stores the most delicate, and the most fleeting impressions.

As I walked home through St James's Park, the dawn was just breaking over London. The swans were lying asleep on the smooth surface of the polished lake, like white feathers fallen upon a mirror of black steel. The gaunt Palace looked purple against the pale-green sky, and in the garden of Stafford House the birds were just beginning to sing. I thought of Cyril Graham, and my eyes filled with tears.

## 2

It was past twelve o'clock when I awoke, and the sun was streaming in through the curtains of my room in long dusty beams of tremulous gold. I told my servant that I would not be at home to anyone, and after I had discussed a cup of chocolate and a *petit-pain*, I took out of the library my copy of Shakespeare's Sonnets, and Mr. Tyler's facsimile edition of the Quarto, and began to go carefully through them. Each poem seemed to me to corroborate Cyril Graham's theory. I felt as if I had my hand upon Shakespeare's heart, and was counting each separate throb and pulse of passion. I thought of the wonderful boy-actor, and saw his face in every line.

Previous to this, in my Lord Pembroke days, if I may so term them, I must admit that it had always seemed to me very difficult to understand how the creator of Hamlet and Lear and Othello could have addressed in such extravagant terms of praise and passion one who was merely an ordinary young nobleman of the day. Along with most students of Shakespeare, I had found myself compelled to set the Sonnets apart as things quite alien to Shakespeare's development as a dramatist, as things possibly unworthy of the intellectual side of his nature. But now that I began to realise the truth of Cyril Graham's theory, I saw that the moods and passions they mirrored were absolutely essential to Shakespeare's perfection as an artist writing for the Elizabethan stage, and that it was in the curious theatric conditions of that stage that the poems themselves had their origin. I remember what joy I had in feeling that these wonderful Sonnets,

> Subtle as Sphinx; as sweet and musical
> As bright Apollo's lute, strung with his hair,

were no longer isolated from the great aesthetic energies of Shakespeare's life but were an essential part of his dramatic activity, and revealed to us something of the secret of his method. To have discovered the true name of Mr. W. H. was comparatively nothing: others might have done that, had perhaps done it: but to have discovered his profession was a revolution in criticism.

Two sonnets, I remember, struck me particularly. In the first of these (53), Shakespeare, complimenting Willie Hughes on the versatility of his acting, on his wide range of parts, a range extending, as we know, from Rosalind to Juliet, and from Beatrice to Ophelia, says to him—

> What is your substance, whereof are you made,
> That millions of strange shadows on you tend?
> Since every one hath, every one, one shade,
> And you, but one, can every shadow lend—

lines that would be unintelligible if they were not addressed to an actor, for the word "shadow" had in Shakespeare's day a technical meaning connected with the stage. "The best in this kind are but shadows," says Theseus of the actors in the *Midsummer Night's Dream*;

> Life's but a walking shadow, a poor player
> That struts and frets his hour upon the stage,

cries Macbeth in the moment of his despair, and there are many similar allusions in the literature of the day. This sonnet evidently belonged to the series in which Shakespeare discusses the nature of the actor's art, and of the strange and rare temperament that is essential to the perfect stage-player. "How is it," says Shakespeare to Willie Hughes, "that you have so many personalities?" and then he goes on to point out that his beauty is such that it seems to realise every form and phase of fancy, to embody each dream of the creative imagination—an idea that is still further expanded in the sonnet that immediately follows, where, beginning with the fine thought,

> O, how much more doth beauty beauteous seem
> By that sweet ornament which *truth* doth give!

Shakespeare invites us to notice how the truth of acting, the truth of visible presentation on the stage, adds to the wonder of poetry, giving life to its loveliness, and actual reality to its ideal form. And yet, in Sonnet 67, Shakespeare calls upon Willie Hughes to abandon the stage with its artificiality, its unreal life of painted face and mimic costume, its immoral influences and suggestions, its remoteness from the true world of noble action and sincere utterance.

> Ah! wherefore with infection should he live,
> And with his presence grace impiety,
> That sin by him advantage should achieve
> And lace itself with his society?
> Why should false painting imitate his cheek,
> And steal dead seeming of his living hue?
> Why should poor beauty indirectly seek
> Roses of shadow, since his rose is true?

It may seem strange that so great a dramatist as Shakespeare, who realised his own perfection as an artist and his full humanity as a man on the ideal plane of stage-writing and stage-playing, should have written in these terms about the theatre; but we must remember that in Sonnets 110 and 111, Shakespeare shows us that he too was wearied of the world of puppets, and full of shame at having made himself "a motley to the view." Sonnet 111 is especially bitter—

> O, for my sake do you with Fortune chide,
> The guilty goddess of my harmful deeds,
> That did not better for my life provide
> Than public means which public manners breeds.
> Thence comes it that my name receives a brand,
> And almost thence my nature is subdued
> To what it works in, like the dyer's hand.
> Pity me, then, and wish I were renewed—

and there are many signs of the same feeling elsewhere, signs familiar to all real students of Shakespeare.

One point puzzled me immensely as I read the Sonnets, and it was days before I struck on the true interpretation, which indeed Cyril Graham himself seems to have missed. I could not understand how it was that Shakespeare set so high a value on his young friend marrying. He himself had married young and the result had been unhappiness, and it was not likely that he would have asked Willie Hughes to commit the same error. The boy-player of Rosalind had nothing to gain from marriage, or from the passions of real life. The early sonnets with their strange entreaties to have children seemed to be a jarring note.

The explanation of the mystery came on me quite suddenly, and I found it in the curious dedication. It will be remembered that this dedication runs as follows—

TO.THE.ONLIE.BEGETTER.OF.
THESE.INSUING.SONNETS.
MR. W. H. ALL.HAPPINESSE.
AND.THAT.ETERNITIE.
PROMISED.BY.
OUR.EVER-LIVING.POET.
WISHETH.
THE.WELL-WISHING.
ADVENTURER.IN.
SETTING.
FORTH.

T. T.

Some scholars have supposed that the word "begetter" here means simply the procurer of the Sonnets for Thomas Thorpe the publisher; but this view is now generally abandoned, and the highest authorities are quite agreed that it is to be taken in the sense of inspirer, the metaphor being drawn from the analogy of physical life. Now I saw that the same metaphor was used by Shakespeare himself all through the poems, and this set me on the right track. Finally I made my great discovery. The marriage that Shakespeare proposes for Willie Hughes is the "marriage with his Muse," an expression which is definitely put forward in Sonnet 82 where, in the bitterness of his heart at the defection of the boy-actor for whom he had written his greatest parts, and whose beauty had indeed suggested them, he opens his complaint by saying—

I grant thou wert not married to my muse.

The children he begs him to beget are no children of flesh and blood, but more immortal children of undying fame. The whole cycle of the early sonnets is simply Shakespeare's invitation to Willie Hughes to go upon the stage and become a player. How barren and profitless a thing, he says, is this beauty of yours if it be not used—

> When forty winters shall besiege thy brow,
> And dig deep trenches in thy beauty's field,
> Thy youth's proud livery, so gazed on now,
> Will be a tattered weed, of small worth held.
> Then being asked where all thy beauty lies,
> Where all the treasure of thy lusty days,
> To say within thine own deep-sunken eyes,
> Were an all-eating shame and thriftless praise.

You must create something in art: my verse "is thine and *born* of thee"; only listen to me, and I will

> *bring forth* eternal numbers to outlive long date,

and you shall people with forms of your own image the imaginary world of the stage. These children that you beget, he continues, will not wither away, as mortal children do, but you shall live in them and in my plays: do but—

> Make thee another self, for love of me,
> That beauty still may live in thine or thee!

Be not afraid to surrender your personality, to give your "semblance to some other":

> To give away yourself keeps yourself still,
> And you must live, drawn by your own sweet skill.

I may not be learned in astrology, and yet, in those "constant stars" your eyes,

> I read such art
> As truth and beauty shall together thrive,
> If from thyself to store thou wouldst convert.

What does it matter about others?

> Let those whom Nature hath not made for store,
> Harsh, featureless, and rude, barrenly perish:

With you it is different, Nature—

> carv'd thee for her seal, and meant thereby
> Thou shouldst print more, nor let that copy die.

Remember, too, how soon Beauty forsakes itself. Its action is no stronger than a flower, and like a flower it lives and dies. Think of "the stormy gusts of winter's day," of the "barren edge of Death's eternal cold," and—

> ere thou be distilled,
> Make sweet some vial; treasure thou some place
> With beauty's treasure, ere it be self-killed.

Why, even flowers do not altogether die. When roses wither,

> Of their sweet deaths are sweetest odours made:

and you who are "my rose" should not pass away without leaving your form in Art. For Art has the very secret of joy.

> Ten times theyself were happier than thou art,
> If ten of thine ten times refigur'd thee.

You do not require the "bastard signs of fair," the painted face, the fantastic disguises of other actors:

> . . . the golden tresses of the dead,
> The right of sepulchres,

need not be shorn away for you. In you—

> . . . those holy antique hours are seen,
> Without all ornament, itself and true,
> Making no summer of another's green.

All that is necessary is to "copy what in you is writ"; to place you on the stage as you are in actual life. All those ancient poets who have written of "ladies dead and lovely knights" have been dreaming of such a one as you, and:

All their praises are but prophecies
Of this our time, all you prefiguring.

For your beauty seems to belong to all ages and to all lands. Your shade comes to visit me at night, but, I want to look upon your "shadow" in the living day, I want to see you upon the stage. Mere description of you will not suffice:

If I could write the beauty of your eyes,
And in fresh numbers number all your graces,
The age to come would say, "This poet lies;
Such heavenly touches ne'er touched earthly faces."

It is necessary that "some child of yours," some artistic creation that embodies you, and to which your imagination gives life, shall present you to the world's wondering eyes. Your own thoughts are your children, offspring of sense and spirit; give some expression to them, and you shall find—

Those children nursed, delivered from thy brain.

My thoughts, also, are my "children." They are of your begetting and my brain is:

the womb wherein they grew.

For this great friendship of ours is indeed a marriage, it is the "marriage of true minds."

I collected together all the passages that seemed to me to corroborate this view, and they produced a strong impression on me, and showed me how complete Cyril Graham's theory really was. I also saw that it was quite easy to separate those lines in which Shakespeare speaks of the Sonnets themselves from those in which he speaks of his great dramatic work. This was a point that had been entirely overlooked by all critics up to Cyril Graham's day. And yet it was one of the most important in the whole series of poems. To the Sonnets Shakespeare was more or less indifferent. He did not wish to rest his fame on them. They were to him his "slight Muse," as he calls them, and intended, as Meres tells us, for private circulation only among a few, a very few, friends. Upon the other hand he was extremely conscious of the high artistic value of his plays, and shows a noble self-reliance upon his dramatic genius.  When he says to Willie Hughes:

> But thy eternal summer shall not fade
> Nor lose possession of that fair thou ow'st,
> Nor shall death brag thou wander'st in his shade,
> When in *eternal lines* to time thou grow'st,
>    So long as men can breathe or eyes can see,
>    So long lives this, and this gives life to thee—

the expression "eternal lines" clearly alludes to one of his plays that he was sending him at the time, just as the concluding couplet points to his confidence in the probability of his plays being always acted.  In his address to the Dramatic Muse (Sonnets 100 and 101), we find the same feeling.

> Where art thou, muse, that thou forget'st so long
> To speak of that which gives thee all thy might?
> Spend'st thou thy fury on some worthless song,
> Darkening thy power to lend base subjects light?

he cries, and he then proceeds to reproach the mistress of Tragedy and Comedy for her "neglect of truth in beauty dyed," and says:

> Because he needs no praise, wilt thou be dumb?
> Excuse not silence so; for't lies in thee
> To make him much outlive a gilded tomb,
> And to be praised of ages yet to be.
>    Then do thy office, muse; I teach thee how,
>    To make him seem long hence as he shows now.

It is, however, perhaps in Sonnet 55 that Shakespeare gives to this idea its fullest expression.  To imagine that the "powerful rhyme" of the second line refers to the sonnet itself was entirely to mistake Shakespeare's meaning.  It seemed to me that it was extremely likely, from the general character of the sonnet, that a particular play was meant, and that the play was none other but *Romeo and Juliet*.

> Not marble nor the gilded monuments
> Of princes shall outlive this powerful rhyme,
> But you shall shine more bright in these contents
> That unswept stone besmeared with sluttish time.
> When wasteful wars shall statues overturn,

And broils root out the work of masonry,
Nor Mars his sword nor wars quick fire shall burn
The living record of your memory.
'Gainst death and all oblivious enmity
Shall you pace forth; your praise shall still find room
Even in the eyes of all posterity
That wear this world out to the ending doom.
    So, till the judgment that yourself arise,
    You live in this, and dwell in lovers' eyes.

It was also very suggestive to note how here as elsewhere Shakespeare promised Willie Hughes immortality in a form that appealed to men's eyes—that is to say, in a spectacular form, in a play that is to be looked at.

For two weeks I worked hard at the Sonnets, hardly ever going out, and refusing all invitations. Every day I seemed to be discovering something new, and Willie Hughes became to me a kind of spiritual presence, an ever-dominant personality. I could almost fancy that I saw him standing in the shadow of my room, so well had Shakespeare drawn him, with his golden hair, his tender flower-like grace, his dreamy deep-sunken eyes, his delicate mobile limbs, and his white lily hands. His very name fascinated me. Willie Hughes! Willie Hughes! How musically it sounded! Yes; who else but he could have been the master-mistress of Shakespeare's passion (20:2), the lord of his love to whom he was bound in vassalage (26:1), the delicate minion of pleasure (126:9), the rose of the whole world (109:14), the herald of the spring (1:10) decked in the proud livery of youth (2:3), the lovely boy whom it was sweet music to hear (8:1), and whose beauty was the very raiment of Shakespeare's heart (2:6), as it was the keystone of his dramatic power? How bitter now seemed the whole tragedy of his desertion and his shame!—shame that he made sweet and lovely (95:1) by the mere magic of his personality, but that was none the less shame. Yet as Shakespeare forgave him, should not we forgive him also? I did not care to pry into the mystery of his sin or of the sin, if such it was, of the great poet who had so dearly loved him. "I am that I am," said Shakespeare in a sonnet of noble scorn—

I am that I am, and they that level
At my abuses reckon up their own;
I may be straight, though they themselves be bevel;
By their rank thoughts my deeds must not be shown.

Willie Hughes's abandonment of Shakespeare's theatre was a different matter, and I investigated it at great length. Finally I came to the conclusion that Cyril Graham had been wrong in regarding the rival dramatist of Sonnet 80 as Chapman. It was obviously Marlowe who was alluded to. At the time the Sonnets were written, which must have been between 1590 and 1595, such an expression as "the proud full sail of his great verse" could not have been used of Chapman's work, however applicable it might have been to the style of his later Jacobean plays. No; Marlowe was clearly the rival poet of whom Shakespeare spoke in such laudatory terms; the hymn he wrote in Willie Hughes's honour was the unfinished *Hero and Leander*, and that

> affable familiar ghost
> Which nightly gulls him with intelligence,

was the Mephistopheles of his *Doctor Faustus*. No doubt, Marlowe was fascinated by the beauty and grace of the boy-actor, and lured him away from the Blackfriars Theatre, that he might play the Gaveston of his *Edward II*. That Shakespeare had the legal right to retain Willie Hughes in his own company is evident from Sonnet 87, where he says:

> Farewell—thou art too dear for my possessing,
> And like enough thou know'st thy estimate.
> The *charter of thy worth* gives thee releasing;
> My *bonds* in thee are all determinate.
> For how do I hold thee but by thy granting,
> And for that riches where is my deserving?
> The cause of this fair gift in me is wanting,
> *And so my patent back again is swerving.*
> Thyself thou gav'st, thy own worth then not knowing,
> Or me to whom thou gav'st it, else mistaking;
> So thy great gift, upon misprision growing,
> Comes note again, on better judgment making.
> > Thus have I had thee, as a dream doth flatter,
> > In sleep a king, but waking no such matter.

But him whom he could not hold by love, he would not hold by force. Willie Hughes became a member of Lord Pembroke's company, and perhaps in the open yard of the Red Bull Tavern, played the part of King Edward's delicate minion. On Marlowe's death, he seems to have returned to Shakespeare, who, whatever his fellow-partners may have thought of the matter, was not slow to forgive the willfulness and treachery of the young actor.

How well, too, had Shakespeare drawn the temperament of the stage-player! Willie Hughes was one of those—

> That do not do the thing they most do show,
> Who, moving others, are themselves as stone.

He could act love, but could not feel it, could mimic passion without realising it.

> In many's looks the false heart's history
> Is writ it moods and frowns and wrinkles strange,

but with Willie Hughes it was not so. "Heaven," says Shakespeare, in a sonnet of mad idolatry—

> Heaven in thy creation did decree
> That in thy face sweet love should ever dwell;
> Whate'er thy thoughts or thy heart's workings be,
> Thy looks should nothing thence but sweetness tell.

In his "inconstant mind" and his "false heart" it was easy to recognise the insincerity and treachery that somehow seem inseparable from the artistic nature, as in his love of praise, that desire for immediate recognition that characterises all actors. And yet, more fortunate in this than other actors, Willie Hughes was to know something of immortality. Intimately connected with Shakespeare's plays, he was to live in them, and by their production.

> Your name from hence immortal life shall have,
> Though I, once gone, to all the world must die:
> The earth can yield me but a common grave,
> When you entombed in men's eyes shall lie.
> Your monument shall he my gentle verse,
> Which eyes not yet created shall o'er-read,
> And tongues to be your being shall rehearse,
> When all the breathers of this world are dead.

Nash with his venomous tongue had railed against Shakespeare for "reposing eternity in the mouth of a player," the reference being obviously to the Sonnets.

But to Shakespeare, the actor was a deliberate and self-conscious fellow worker who gave form and substance to a poet's fancy, and brought into Drama the elements of a noble realism. His silence could be as eloquent as words, and his gestures as expressive, and in those terrible moments of Titan agony or of god-like pain, when thought outstrips utterance, when the soul sick with excess of anguish stammers or is dumb, and the very raiment of speech is rent and torn by passion in its storm, then the actor could become, though it were but for a moment, a creative artist, and touch by his mere presence and personality those springs of terror and of pity to which tragedy appeals. This full recognition of the actor's art, and of the actor's power, was one of the things that distinguished the Romantic from the Classical Drama, and one of the things, consequently, that we owed to Shakespeare, who, fortunate in much, was fortunate also in this, that he was able to find Richard Burbage and to fashion Willie Hughes.

With what pleasures he dwelt upon Willie Hughes' influence over his audience—the "gazers" as he calls them; with what charm of fancy did he analyse the whole art! Even in the "Lover's Complaint" he speaks of his acting, and tells us that he was a nature so impressionable to the quality of dramatic situations that he could assume "all strange forms"—

> Of burning blushes, or of weeping water,
> Or swooning paleness:

explaining his meaning more fully later on where he tells us how Willie Hughes was able to deceive others by his wonderful power to—

> Blush at speeches rank, to weep at woes,
> Or to turn white and swoon at tragic shows.

It had never been pointed out before that the shepherd of this lovely pastoral, whose "youth in art and art in youth" are described with such subtlety of phrase and passion, was none other than the Mr. W. H. of the Sonnets. And yet there was no doubt that he was so. Not merely in personal appearance are the two lads the same, but their natures and temperaments are identical. When the false shepherd whispers to the fickle maid—

> All my offenses that abroad you see
> Are errors of the blood, none of the mind;
> Love made them not:

when he says of his lovers,

> Harm have I done to them, but ne'er was harmed;
> Kept hearts in liveries, but mine own was free,
> And reigned, commanding in his monarchy:

when he tells us of the "deep-brained sonnets" that one of them had sent him, and cries out in boyish pride—

> The broken bosoms that to me belong
> Have emptied all their fountains in my well:

it is impossible not to feel that it is Willie Hughes who is speaking to us. "Deep-brained sonnets," indeed, had Shakespeare brought him, "jewels" that to his careless eyes were but as "trifles," though—

> Each several stone,
> With wit well blazoned, smiled or made some moan;

and into the well of beauty he had emptied the sweet fountain of his song. That in both places it was an actor who was alluded to, was also clear. The betrayed nymph tells us of the "false fire" in her lover's cheek, of the "forced thunder" of his sighs, and of his "borrowed motion": of whom, indeed, but of an actor could it be said that to him "thought, characters, and words" were "merely Art," or that—

> To make the weeper laugh, the laugher weep,
> He had the dialect and the different skill,
> Catching all passions in his craft of will?

The play on words in the last line is the same as that used in the punning sonnets, and is continued in the following stanza of the poem, where we are told of the youth who—

> did in the general bosom reign
> Of young, of old; and sexes both enchanted,

that there were those who—

> . . . dialogued for him what he would say,
> Asked their own wills, and made their Wills obey.

Yes: the "rose-cheeked Adonis" of the Venus poem, the false shepherd of the "Lover's Complaint," the "tender churl," the "beauteous niggard" of the Sonnets, was none other but a young actor; and as I read through the various descriptions given of him, I saw that the love that Shakespeare bore him was as the love of a musician for some delicate instrument on which he delights to play, as a sculptor's love for some rare and exquisite material that suggests a new form of plastic beauty, a new mode of plastic expression. For all Art has its medium, its material, be that of rhythmical words, or of pleasurable colour, or of sweet and subtly-divided sound; and, as one of the most fascinating critics of our day has pointed out, it is to the qualities inherent in each material, and special to it, that we owe the sensuous element in Art, and with it all that in Art is essentially artistic. What then shall we say of the material that the Drama requires for its perfect presentation? What of the Actor, who is the medium through which alone the Drama can truly reveal itself? Surely, in that strange mimicry of life by the living which is the mode and method of theatric art, there are sensuous elements of beauty that none of the other arts possess. Looked at from one point of view, the common players of the saffron-strewn stage are Art's most complete, most satisfying instruments. There is no passion in bronze, nor motion in marble. The sculptor must surrender colour, and the painter fullness of form. The epos changes acts into words, and music changes words into tones. It is the Drama only that, to quote the fine saying of Gervinus, uses all means at once, and, appealing both to eye and ear, has at its disposal, and in its service, form and colour, tone, look, and word, the swiftness of motion, the intense realism of visible action.

It may be that in this very completeness of the instrument lies the secret of some weakness in the art. Those arts are happiest that employ a material remote from reality, and there is a danger in the absolute identity of medium and matter, the danger of ignoble realism and unimaginative imitation. Yet Shakespeare himself was a player, and wrote for players. He saw the possibilities that lay hidden in an art that up to his time had expressed itself but in bombast or in clowning. He has left us the most perfect rules for acting that have ever been written. He created parts that can be only truly revealed to us on the stage, wrote plays that need theatre for their full realisation, and we cannot marvel that he so worshipped one who was the interpreter of his vision, as he was the incarnation of his dreams.

There was, however, more in his friendship than the mere delight of a dramatist in one who helps him to achieve his end. This was indeed a subtle element of pleasure, if not of passion, and a noble basis for artistic comradeship. But it was not all that the Sonnets revealed to us. There was something beyond. There was the soul, as well as the language, of neo-Platonism.

"The fear of the Lord is the beginning of wisdom," said the stern Hebrew prophet: "The beginning of wisdom is Love," was the gracious message of the Greek. And the spirit of the Renaissance, which already touched Hellenism at so many points, catching the inner meaning of this phrase and divining its secret, sought to elevate friendship to the high dignity of the antique ideal, to make it a vital factor in the new culture, and a mode of self-conscious intellectual development. In 1492 appeared Marsilio Ficino's translation of the "Symposium" of Plato, and his wonderful dialogue, of all the Platonic dialogues perhaps the most perfect, as it is the most poetical, began to exercise a strange influence over men, and to colour their words and thoughts, and manner of living. In its subtle suggestions of sex in soul, in the curious analogies it draws between intellectual enthusiasm and the physical passion of love, in its dream of the incarnation of the Idea in a beautiful and living form, and of a real spiritual conception with a travail and a bringing to birth, there was something that fascinated the poets and scholars of the sixteenth century. Shakespeare, certainly, was fascinated by it, and had read the dialogue, if not in Ficino's translation, of which many copies found their way to England, perhaps in that French translation by Leroy to which Joachim du Bellay contributed so many graceful metrical versions. When he says to Willie Hughes,

> he that calls on thee, let him bring forth
> Eternal numbers to outlive long date,

he is thinking of Diotima's theory that Beauty is the goddess who presides over birth, and draws into the light of day the dim conceptions of the soul: when he tells us of the "marriage of true minds," and exhorts his friend to beget children that time cannot destroy, he is but repeating the words in which the prophetess tells us that "friends are married by a far nearer tie than those who beget mortal children, for fairer and more immortal are the children who are their common offspring." So, also, Edward Blount in his dedication of *Hero and Leander* talks of Marlowe's works as his "right children," being the "issue of his brain"; and when Bacon claims that "the best works and of greatest merit for the public have proceeded from the unmarried and childless men, which both in affection and means have married and endowed the public," he is paraphrasing a passage in the "Symposium."

Friendship, indeed, could have desired no better warrant for its permanence or its ardours than the Platonic theory, or creed, as we might better call it, that the true world was the world of ideas, and that these ideas took form and became incarnate in man, and it is only when we realise the influence of neo-Platonism on the Renaissance that we can understand the true meaning of the amatory phrases and words with which friends were wont, at this time, to address each other. There was a kind of mystic transference of the expressions of the physical world to a sphere that was spiritual, that was removed from gross bodily appetite, and in which the soul was Lord. Love had, indeed, entered the olive garden of the new Academe, but he wore the same flame-coloured raiment, and had the same words of passion on his lips.

Michael Angelo, the "haughtiest spirit in Italy," as he has been called, addresses the young Tommaso Cavalieri in such fervent and passionate terms that some have thought that the sonnets in question must have been intended for that noble lady, the widow of the Marchese di Pescara, whose white hand, when she was dying, the great sculptor's lips had stooped to kiss. But that it was to Cavalieri that they were written, and that the literal interpretation is the right one, is evident not merely from the fact that Michael Angelo plays with his name, as Shakespeare plays with the name of Willie Hughes, but from the direct evidence of Varchi, who was well acquainted with the young man, and who, indeed, tells us that he possessed "besides incomparable personal beauty, so much charm of nature, such excellent abilities, and such a graceful manner, that he deserved, and still deserves, to be the better loved the more he is known." Strange as these sonnets may seem to us now, when rightly interpreted they merely serve to show with what intense and religious fervour Michael Angelo addressed himself to the worship of intellectual beauty, and how, to borrow a fine phrase from Mr. Symonds, he pierced through the veil of flesh and sought the divine idea it imprisoned. In the sonnet written for Luigi del Riccio on the death of his friend, Cecchino Bracci, we can also trace, as Mr. Symonds points out, the Platonic conception of love as nothing if not spiritual, and of beauty as a form that finds its im-

mortality within the lover's soul. Cecchino was a lad who died at the
age of seventeen, and when Luigi asked Michael Angelo to make a
portrait of him, Michael Angelo answered, "I can only do so by draw-
ing you in whom he still lives."

> If the beloved in the lover shine,
> Since Art without him cannot work alone,
> Thee must I carve, to tell the world of him.

The same idea is also put forward in Montaigne's noble essay on
Friendship, a passion which he ranks higher than the love of brother
for brother, or the love of man for woman. He tells us—I quote from
Florio's translation, one of the books with which Shakespeare was
familiar—how "perfect amitie" is indivisible, how it "possesseth the
soule, and swaies it in all soveraigntie," and how "by the interposition
of a spiritual beauty the desire of a spiritual conception is engendered
in the beloved." He writes of an "internall beauty, of difficile knowl-
edge, and abstruse discovery" that is revealed unto friends, and unto
friends only. He mourns for the dead Etienne de la Boëtie, in accents
of wild grief and inconsolable love. The learned Hubert Languet, the
friend of Melanchthon and of the leaders of the reformed church,
tells the young Philip Sidney how he kept his portrait by him some
hours to feast his eyes upon it, and how his appetite was "rather in-
creased than diminished by the sight," and Sidney writes to him, "the
chief hope of my life, next to the everlasting blessedness of heaven,
will always be the enjoyment of true friendship, and there you shall
have the chiefest place." Later on there came to Sidney's house in
London, one—some day to be burned at Rome, for the sin of seeing
God in all things—Giordano Bruno, just fresh from his triumph be-
fore the University of Paris. "A filosofia è necessario amore" were the
words ever upon his lips, and there was something in his strange ar-
dent personality that made men feel that he had discovered the new
secret of life. Ben Jonson writing to one of his friends subscribes him-
self "your true lover," and dedicates his noble eulogy on Shakespeare
"To the memory of my Beloved." Richard Barnfield in his "Affection-
ate Shepherd" flutes on soft Virgilian reed the story of his attachment
to some young Elizabethan of the day. Out of all the *Eclogues*, Abraham
Fraunce selects the second for translation, and Fletcher's lines to Master
W. C. show what fascination was hidden in the mere name of Alexis.
    It was no wonder then that Shakespeare had been stirred by a spirit

that so stirred his age. There had been critics, like Hallam, who had regretted that the Sonnets had ever been written, who had seen in them something dangerous, something unlawful even. To them it would have been sufficient to answer in Chapman's noble words:

> There is no danger to a man that knows
> What Life and Death is: there's not any law
> Exceeds his knowledge: neither is it lawful
> That he should stoop to nay other law.

But it was evident that the Sonnets needed no such defence as this, and that those who had talked of "the folly of excessive and misplaced affection" had not been able to interpret either the language or the spirit of these great poems, so intimately connected with the philosophy and the art of their time. It is no doubt true that to be filled with an absorbing passion is to surrender the security of one's lower life, and yet in such surrender there may be gain, certainly there was for Shakespeare. When Pico della Mirandola crossed the threshold of the villa of Careggi, and stood before Marsilio Ficino in all the grace and comeliness of his wonderful youth, the aged scholar seemed to see in him the realisation of the Greek ideal, and determined to devote his remaining years to the translation of Plotinus, that new Plato, in whom, as Mr. Pater reminds us, "the mystical element in the Platonic philosophy had been worked out to the utmost limit of vision and ecstasy." A romantic friendship with a young Roman of his day initiated Winckelmann into the secret of Greek art, taught him the mystery of its beauty and the meaning of its form. In Willie Hughes, Shakespeare found not merely a most delicate instrument for the presentation of his art, but the visible incarnation of his idea of beauty, and it is not too much to say that to this young actor, whose very name the dull writers of his age forgot to chronicle, the Romantic Movement of English Literature is largely indebted.

### 3

One evening I thought that I had really found Willie Hughes in Elizabethan literature. In a wonderfully graphic account of the last days of the great Earl of Essex, his chaplain Thomas Knell, tells us that the night before the Earl died, "he called William Hewes, which was his musician, to play upon the virginals and to sing. 'Play,' said he, 'my song, Will Hewes, and I will sing it to myself.' So he did it most joyfully, not as the howling swan, which, still looking down, waileth her end, but as a sweet lark, lifting up his hands and casting up his eyes to his God, with this mounted the crystal skies, and reached with his unwearied tongue the top of highest heavens." Surely the boy who played on the virginals to the dying father of Sidney's Stella was none other but the Will Hews to whom Shakespeare dedicated the Sonnets, and whom he tells us was himself sweet "music to hear." Yet Lord Essex died in 1576, when Shakespeare himself was but twelve years of age. It was impossible that his musician could have been the Mr. W. H. of the Sonnets. Perhaps Shakespeare's young friend was the son of the player upon the virginals? It was at least something to have discovered that Will Hews was an Elizabethan name. Indeed the name Hews seemed to have been closely connected with music and the stage. The first English actress was the lovely Margaret Hews, whom Prince Rupert so madly adored. What more probable than that between her and Lord Essex's musician had come the boy-actor of Shakespeare's plays? In 1587 a certain Thomas Hewes brought out at Gray's Inn a Euripidean tragedy entitled *The Misfortunes of Arthur*, receiving much assistance in the arrangement of the dumb shows from one Francis Bacon, then a student of law. Surely he was some near kinsman of the lad to whom Shakespeare said—

Take all my loves, my love, yea, take them all;

the "profitless usurer?" of "unused beauty," as he describes him. But the proofs, the links—where were they? Alas! I could not find them. It seemed to me that I was always on the brink of absolute verification, but that I could never really attain to it. I thought it strange that no one had ever written a history of the English boy-actors of the sixteenth and seventeenth centuries, and determined to undertake the task myself, and to try to ascertain their true relations to the drama. The subject was, certainly, full of artistic interest. These lads had been the delicate reeds through which our poets had sounded their sweetest strains, the gracious vessels of honour into which they had poured the purple wine of their song. Foremost, naturally, among them all had been the youth to whom Shakespeare had intrusted the realisation of his most exquisite creations. Beauty had been his, such as our age has never, or but rarely seen, a beauty that seemed to combine the charm of both sexes, and to have wedded, as the Sonnets tell us, the grace of Adonis and the loveliness of Helen. He had been quick-witted, too, and eloquent, and from those finely curved lips that the satirist had mocked at had come the passionate cry of Juliet, and the bright laughter of Beatrice, Perdita's flower-like words, and Ophelia's wandering songs. Yet as Shakespeare himself had been but as a God among giants, so Willie Hughes had only been one out of many marvellous lads to whom our English Renaissance owed something of the secret of its joy, and it appeared to me that they also were worthy of some study and record.

In a little book with fine vellum leaves and damask silk cover—a fancy of mine in those fanciful days—I accordingly collected such information as I could about them, and even now there is something in the scanty record of their lives, in the mere mention of their names, that attracts me. I seemed to know them all: Robin Armin, the goldsmith's lad who was lured by Tarlton to go on the stage: Sandford, whose performance of the courtezan Flamantia Lord Burleigh witnessed at Gray's Inn: Cooke, who played Agrippina in the tragedy of *Sejanus*: Nat. Field, whose young and beardless portrait is still preserved for us at Dulwich, and who in *Cynthia's Revels* played the "Queen and Huntress chaste and fair": Gil Carie, who, attired as a mountain nymph, sang in the same lovely masque Echo's song of mourning for Narcissus: Parsons, the Salmacis of the strange pageant of *Tamburlaine*: Will. Ostler, who was one of "The Children of the Queen's Chapel," and accompanied King James to Scotland: George Vernon, to whom the king sent a cloak of scarlet, cloth, and a cape of crimson velvet: Alick Gough, who performed the part of Cænis, Vespasian's concubine, in Massinger's *Roman Actor*, and three years later that of Acanthe, in the same dramatist's *Picture*: Barrett, the heroine of Richards' tragedy of *Messalina*: Dicky Robinson, "a very pretty fellow," Ben Jonson tells us, who was a member of Shakespeare's company, and was known for his exquisite taste in costume, as well as for his love of woman's apparel: Salathiel Pavy, whose early and tragic death Jonson mourned in one of the sweetest threnodies of our literature: Arthur Savile, who was one of "the players of Prince Charles," and took a girl's part in a comedy by Marmion: Stephen Hammerton, "a most noted and beautiful woman actor," whose pale oval face with its heavy-lidded eyes and somewhat sensuous mouth looks out at us from a curious miniature of the time: Hart, who made his first success by playing the Duchess in the tragedy of *The Cardinal*, and who in a poem that is clearly mod-

elled upon some of Shakespeare's Sonnets is described by one who
had seen him as "beauty to the eye, and music to the ear": and Kynaston,
of whom Betterton said that "it has been disputed among the judi-
cious, whether any woman could have more sensibly touched the pas-
sions," and whose white hands and amber-coloured hair seem to have
retarded by some years the introduction of actresses upon our stage.

The Puritans, with their uncouth morals and ignoble minds had
of course railed against them, and dwelt on the impropriety of boys
disguising as women, and learning to affect the manners and passions
of the female sex. Gosson, with his shrill voice, and Prynne, soon to
be made earless for many shameful slanders, and others to whom the
rare and subtle sense of abstract beauty was denied, had from the
pulpit and through pamphlet said foul or foolish things to their
dishonour. To Francis Lenton, writing in 1629, what he speaks of as—

> loose action, mimic gesture
> By a poor boy clad in a princely vesture,

is but one of many—

> tempting baits of hell
> Which draw more youth unto the damned cell
> Of furious lust, than all the devil could do
> Since he obtained his first overthrow.

Deuteronomy was quoted and the ill-digested learning of the period
laid under contribution. Even our own time had not appreciated the
artistic conditions of the Elizabethan and Jacobean drama. One of
the most brilliant and intellectual actresses of this century had laughted
at the idea of a lad of seventeen or eighteen playing Imogen, or Miranda,
or Rosalind. "How could any youth, however gifted and specially
trained, even faintly suggest these fair and noble women to an
audience? . . . One quite pities Shakespeare, who had to put up with
seeing his brightest creations marred, misrepresented, and spoiled."
In his book on *Shakespeare's Predecessors* Mr. John Addington Symonds
also had talked of "hobbledehoys" trying to represent the pathos of
Desdemona and Juliet's passion. Were they right? Are they right? I did
not think so then. I do not think so now. Those who remember the
Oxford production of the *Agamemnon*, the fine utterance and marble
dignity of the Clytemnestra, the romantic and imaginative rendering
of the prophetic madness of Cassandra, will not agree with Lady Mar-

tin or Mr. Symonds in their strictures on the conditions of the Eliza-
bethan stage.

Of all the motives of dramatic curiosity used by our great play-
wrights, there is none more subtle or more fascinating than the ambi-
guity of the sexes. This idea, invented, as far as an artistic idea can be
said to be invented, by Lyly, perfected and made exquisite for us by
Shakespeare, seems to me to owe its origin, as it certainly owes its
possibility of life-like presentation, to the circumstance that the Eliza-
bethan stage, like the stage of the Greeks, admitted the appearance of
no female performers. It is because Lyly was writing for the boy-actors
of St. Paul's that we have the confused sexes and complicated loves of
Phillida and Gallathea: it is because Shakespeare was writing for Willie
Hughes that Rosalind dons doublet and hose, and calls herself
Ganymede, that Viola and Julia put on pages' dress, that Imogen steals
away in male attire. To say that only a woman can portray the passions
of a woman, and that therefore no boy can play Rosalind, is to rob the
art of acting of all claim to objectivity, and to assign to the mere acci-
dent of sex what properly belongs to imaginative insight and creative
energy. Indeed, if sex be an element in artistic creation, it might rather
be urged that the delightful combination of wit and romance which
characterises so many of Shakespeare's heroines was at least occasioned
if it was not actually caused by the fact that the players of these parts
were lads and young men, whose passionate purity, quick mobile fancy,
and healthy freedom from sentimentality can hardly fail to have sug-
gested a new and delightful type of girlhood or of womanhood. The
very difference of sex between the player and the part he represented
must also, as Professor Ward points out, have constituted "one more
demand upon the imaginative capacities of the spectators," and must
have kept them from that over-realistic identification of the actor with
his *rôle*, which is one of the weak points in modern theatrical criticism.

This, too, must be granted, that it was to these boy-actors that we
owe the introduction of those lovely lyrics that star the plays of
Shakespeare, Dekker, and so many of the dramatists of the period,
those "snatches of bird-like or god-like song," as Mr. Swinburne calls
them. For it was out of the choirs of the cathedrals and royal chapels
of England that most of these lads came, and from their earliest years
they had been trained in the singing of anthems and madrigals, and
in all that concerns the subtle art of music. Chosen at first for the
beauty of their voices, as well as for a certain comeliness and freshness
of appearance, they were then instructed in gesture, dancing, and elo-

cution, and taught to play both tragedies and comedies in the English as well as in the Latin language. Indeed, acting seems to have formed part of the ordinary education of the time, and to have been much studied not merely by the scholars of Eton and Westminster, but also by the students at the Universities of Oxford and Cambridge, some of whom went afterwards upon the public stage, as is becoming not uncommon in our own day. The great actors, too, had their pupils and apprentices, who were formally bound over to them by legal warrant, to whom they imparted the secrets of their craft, and who were so much valued that we read of Henslowe, one of the managers of the Rose Theatre, buying a trained boy of the name of James Bristowe for eight pieces of gold. The relations that existed between the masters and their pupils seem to have been of the most cordial and affectionate character. Robin Armin was looked upon by Tarlton as his adopted son, and in a will dated "the fourth daie of Maie. Anno Domini 1605," Augustine Phillips, Shakespeare's dear friend and fellow actor, bequeathed to one of his apprentices his "Purple cloke, sword, and dager," his "base viall," and much rich apparel, and to another a sum of money and many beautiful instruments of music, "to be delivered unto him at the expiration of his terme of yeres in his indenture of apprenticehood." Now and then, when some daring actor kidnapped a boy for the stage, there was an outcry or an investigation. In 1600, for instance, a certain Norfolk gentleman of the name of Henry Clifton came to live in London in order that his son, then about thirteen years of age, might have the opportunity of attending the Bluecoat School, and from a petition which he presented to the Star Chamber, and which has been recently brought to light by Mr. Greenstreet, we learn that as the boy was walking quietly to Christ Church cloister one winter morning he was waylaid by James Robinson, Henry Evans, and Nathaniel Giles, and carried off to the Blackfriars Theatre, "amongste a companie of lewde and dissolute mercenarie players," as his father calls them, in order that he might be trained "in acting of parts in base playes and enterludes." Hearing of his son's misadventure, Mr. Clifton went down at once to the theatre, and demanded his surrender, but "the sayd Nathaniel Giles, James Robinson and Henry Evans most arrogantlie then and there answered that they had authoritie sufficient soe to take any noble man's sonne in this land," and handing the young schoolboy "a scrolle of paper, conteyning parte of one of their said playes and enterludes," commanded him to learn it by heart. Through a warrant issued by Sir John Fortescue, however, the boy was restored to his father the next day, and Court of Star Chamber seems to have suspended or cancelled Evans' privileges.

The fact is that, following a precedent set by Richard III, Elizabeth had issued a commission authorising certain persons to impress into her service all boys who had beautiful voices that they might sing for her in her Chapel Royal, and Nathaniel Giles, her Chief Commissioner, finding that he could deal profitably with the managers of the Globe Theatre, agreed to supply them with personable and graceful lads for the playing of female parts, under colour of taking them for the Queen's service. The actors, accordingly, had a certain amount of legal warrant on their side, and it is interesting to note that many of the boys whom they carried off from their schools or homes, such as Salathiel Pavy, Nat. Field, and Alvery Trussell, became so fascinated by their new art that they attached themselves permanently to the theatre, and would not leave it.

Once it seemed as if girls were to take the place of boys upon the stage, and among the christenings chronicled in the registers of St. Gilles', Crippelgate, occurs the following strange and suggestive entry: "Comedia, base-born, daughter of Alice Bowker and William Johnson, one of the Queen's plaiers, 10 Feb. 1589." But the child upon whom such high hopes had been built died at six years of age, and when, later on, some French actresses came over and played at Blackfriars, we learn that they were "hissed, hooted, and pippin-pelted from the stage." I think that, from what I have said above, we need not regret this in any way. The essentially male culture of the English Renaissance found its fullest and most perfect expression by its own method, and in its own manner.

I remember I used to wonder, at this time, what had been the social position and early life of Willie Hughes before Shakespeare had met him. My investigations into the history of the boy-actors had made me curious of every detail about him. Had he stood in the carved stall of some gilded choir, reading out of a great book painted with square scarlet notes and long black key lines? We know from the Sonnets how clear and pure his voice was, and what skill he had in the art of music. Noble gentlemen, such as the Earl of Leicester and Lord Oxford, had companies of boy-players in their service as part of their household. When Leicester went to the Netherlands in 1585 he brought with him a certain "Will" described as a "plaier." Was this Willie Hughes? Had he acted for Leicester at Kenilworth, and was it there that Shakespeare had first known him? Or was he, like Robin

Armin, simply a lad of low degree but possessing some strange beauty and marvellous fascination? It was evident from the early sonnets that when Shakespeare first came across him he had no connection whatsoever with the stage, and that he was not of high birth has already been shewn. I began to think of him not as the delicate chorister of a Royal Chapel, not as a petted minion trained to sing and dance in Leicester's stately masque, but as some fair-haired English lad whom in one of London's hurrying streets, or on Windsor's green silent meadows, Shakespeare had seen and followed, recognising the artistic possibilities that lay hidden in so comely and gracious a form, and divining by a quick and subtle instant what an actor the lad would make could he be induced to go upon the stage. At this time Willie Hughes' father was dead, as we learn from Sonnet 13, and his mother, whose remarkable beauty he is said to have inherited, may have been induced to allow him to become Shakespeare's apprentice by the fact that boys who played female characters were paid extremely large salaries, larger salaries, indeed, than were given to grown-up actors. Shakespeare's apprentice, at any rate, we know that he became, and we know what a vital factor he was in the development of Shakespeare's art. As a rule, a boy-actor's capacity for representing girlish parts on the stage lasted but for a few years at most. Such characters as Lady Macbeth, Queen Constance and Volumnia, remained of course always within the reach of those who had true dramatic genius and noble presence. Absolute youth was not necessary here, not desirable even. But with Imogen, and Perdita, and Juliet, it was different. "Your beard has begun to grow, and I pray God your voice be not cracked," says Hamlet mockingly to the boy-actor of the strolling company that came to visit him at Elsinore; and certainly when chins grew rough and voices harsh much of the charm and grace of the performance must have gone. Hence comes Shakespeare's passionate pre-occupation with the youth of Willie Hughes, his terror of old age and wasting years, his wild appeal to time to spare the beauty of his friend:

> Make glad and sorry seasons as thou fleet'st,
> And do whate'er thou wilt, swift-footed time,
> To the wide world and all her fading sweets;
> O carve not with the hours my Love's fair brow
> Nor draw no lines there with thine antique pen;
> Him in thy course untainted do allow
> For beauty's pattern to succeeding men.

Time seems to have listened to Shakespeare's prayers, or perhaps Willie Hughes had the secret of perpetual youth. After three years he is quite unchanged:

> To me, fair friend, you never can be old,   ·
> For as you were when first your eye I eyed,
> Such seems your beauty still. Three winters' cold
> Have from the forests shook three summers' pride,
> Three beauteous springs to yellow autumn turned,
> In process of the seasons have I seen,
> Three April perfumes in three hot Junes burned,
> Since first I saw you fresh which yet are green.

More years pass over, and the bloom of his boyhood seems to be still with him. When, in *The Tempest*, Shakespeare, through the lips of Prospero, flung away the wand of his imagination and gave his poetic sovereignty into the weak, graceful hands of Fletcher, it may be that the Miranda who stood wondering by was none other than Willie Hughes himself, and in the last sonnet that his friend addressed to him, the enemy that is feared is not Time but Death.

> O thou, my lovely boy, who in thy power
> Dost hold time's fickle glass, his sickle-hour;
> Who hast by waning grown, and therein show'st
> Thy lovers withering as thy sweet self grow'st—
> If nature, sovereign mistress over wrack,
> As thou goest onwards, still will pluck thee back,
> She keeps thee to this purpose: that her skill
> May time disgrace and wretched minutes kill.
> Yet fear her, O thou minion of her pleasure!
> She may detain but not still keep her treasure.
>     Her audit, though delay'd, answer'd must be,
>     And her quietus is to render thee.

# 4

It was not for some weeks after I had begun my study of the subject that I ventured to approach the curious group of Sonnets (127–152) that deal with the dark woman who, like a shadow or thing of evil omen, came across Shakespeare's great romance, and for a season stood between him and Willie Hughes. They were obviously printed out of their proper place and should have been inserted between Sonnets 33 and 40. Psychological and artistic reasons necessitated this change, a change which I hope will be adopted by all future editors, as without it an entirely false impression is conveyed of the nature and final issue of this noble friendship.

Who was she, this black-browed, olive-skinned woman, with her amorous mouth "that Love's own hand did make," her "cruel eye," and her "foul pride," her strange skill on the virginals and her false, fascinating nature? An over-curious scholar of our day had seen in her a symbol of the Catholic Church, of that Bride of Christ who is "black but comely." Professor Minto, following in the foot-steps of Henry Brown, had regarded the whole group of Sonnets as simply "exercises of skill undertaken in a spirit of wanton defiance and derision of the commonplace." Mr. Gerald Massey, without any historical proof or probability, had insisted that they were addressed to the celebrated Lady Rich, the Stella of Sir Philip Sidney's sonnets, the Philoclea of his *Arcadia*, and that they contained no personal revelation of Shakespeare's life and love, having been written in Lord Pembroke's name and at his request. Mr. Tyler had suggested that they referred to one of Queen Elizabeth's maids-of-honour, by name Mary Fitton. But none of these explanations satisfied the conditions of the problem. The woman that came between Shakespeare and Willie Hughes was a real woman, black-haired, and married, and of evil repute. Lady Rich's fame was evil enough, it is true, but her hair was of—

> fine threads of finest gold,
> In curled knots man's thought to hold,

and her shoulders like "white doves perching." She was, as King James said to her lover, Lord Mountjoy, "a fair woman with a black soul." As for Mary Fitton, we know that she was unmarried in 1601, the time when her amour with Lord Pembroke was discovered, and besides, any theories that connected Lord Pembroke with the Sonnets were, as Cyril Graham had shewn, put entirely out of court by the fact that Lord Pembroke did not come to London till they had been actually written and read by Shakespeare to his friends.

It was not, however, her name that interested me. I was content to hold with Professor Dowden that "To the eyes of no diver among the wrecks of time will that curious talisman gleam." What I wanted to discover was the nature of her influence over Shakespeare, as well as the characteristics of her personality. Two things were certain: she was much older than the poet, and the fascination that she exercised over him was at first purely intellectual. He began by feeling no physical passion for her. "I do not love thee with mine eyes," he says:

> Nor are mine ears with thy tongue's tune delighted;
> Nor tender feeling to base touches prone,
> Nor taste, nor smell, desire to be invited
> To any sensual feast with thee alone.

He did not even think her beautiful:

> My mistress' eyes are nothing like the sun;
> Coral is far more red than her lips' red.
> If snow be white, why then her breasts are dun;
> If hairs be wires, black wires grow on her head.

He had his moments of loathing for her, for, not content with enslaving the soul of Shakespeare, she seems to have sought to snare the senses of Willie Hughes. Then Shakespeare cried aloud—

> Two loves I have of comfort and despair,
> Which like two spirits do suggest me still.
> The better angel is a man right fair,
> The worser spirit a woman coloured ill.
> To win me soon to hell my female evil
> Tempteth my better angel from my side,
> And would corrupt my saint to be a devil,
> Wooing his purity with her foul pride.

Then he sees her as she really is, the "bay where all men ride," the "wide world's common place," the woman who is in the "very refuse" of her evil deeds, and who is "as black as hell, as dark as night." Then it is that he pens that great sonnet upon Lust ("Th'expense of spirit in a waste of shame"), of which Mr. Theodore Watts says rightly that it is the greatest sonnet ever written. And it is then, also, that he offers to mortgage his very life and genius to her if she will but restore to him that "sweetest friend" of whom she had robbed him.

   To compass this end he abandons himself to her, feigns to be full of an absorbing and sensuous passion of possession, forges false words of love, lies to her, and tells her that he lies.

> My thoughts and my discourse as madmen's are,
> At random from the truth vainly express'd;
> For I have sworn thee fair, and thought thee bright,
> Who are as black as hell, as dark as night.

Rather than suffer his friend to be treacherous to him, he will himself be treacherous to his friend. To shield his purity, he will himself be vile. He knew the weakness of the boy-actor's nature, his susceptibility to praise, his inordinate love of admiration, and deliberately set himself to fascinate the woman who had come between them.

It is never with impunity that one's lips say Love's Litany. Words have their mystical power over the soul, and form can create the feeling from which it should have sprung. Sincerity itself, the ardent, momentary sincerity of the artist, is often the unconscious result of style, and in the case of those rare temperaments that are exquisitely susceptible to the influences of language, the use of certain phrases and modes of expression can stir the very pulse of passion, can send the red blood coursing through the veins, and can transform into a strange sensuous energy what in its orgin had been mere æsthetic impulse, and desire of art. So, at least, it seems to have been with Shakespeare. He begins by pretending to love, wears a lover's apparel and has a lover's words upon his lips. What does it matter? It is only acting, only a comedy in real life. Suddenly he finds that what his tongue had spoken his soul had listened to, and that the raiment that he had put on for disguise is a plague-stricken and poisonous thing that eats into his flesh, and that he cannot throw away. Then comes Desire, with its many maladies, and Lust that makes one love all that one loathes, and Shame, with its ashen face and secret smile. He is enthralled by this dark woman, is for a season separated from his friend, and becomes the "vassal-wretch" of one whom he knows to be evil and perverse and unworthy of his love, as of the love of Willie Hughes. "O, from what power," he says—

> hast thou this powerful might
> With insufficiency my heart to sway,
> To make me give the lie to my true sight
> And swear that brightness doth not grace the day?
> Whence hast thou this becoming of things ill,
> That in the very refuse of thy deeds
> There is such strength and warranties of skill
> That in my mind thy worst all best exceeds?

He is keenly conscious of his own degradation, and finally, realising that his genius is nothing to her compared to the physical beauty of the young actor, he cuts with a quick knife the bond that binds him to her, and in this bitter sonnet bids her farewell—

> In loving thee thou know'st I am forsworn,
> But thou art twice forsworn to me love swearing:
> In act thy bed-vow broke, and new faith torn
> In vowing new hate after new love bearing.
> But why of two oaths' breach do I accuse thee
> When I break twenty? I am perjur'd most,
> For all my vows are oaths but to misuse thee,
> And all my honest faith in thee is lost.
> For I have sworn deep oaths of thy deep kindness,
> Oaths of thy love, thy truth, thy constancy,
> And, to enlighten thee, gave eyes to blindness,
> Or made them swear against the thing they see.
>         For I have sworn thee fair—more perjured I,
>         To swear against the truth so foul a lie.

His attitude towards Willie Hughes in the whole matter shews at once the fervour and the self-abnegation of the great love he bore him. There is a poignant touch of pathos in the close of his sonnet:

> Those pretty wrongs that liberty commits,
> When I am sometime absent from thy heart,
> Thy beauty and thy years full well befits,
> For still temptation follows where thou art.
> Gentle thou art, and therefore to be won,
> Beauteous thou art, therefore to be assailed;
> And when a woman woos, what woman's son
> Will sourly leave her till she have prevailed?
> Ay me! But yet thou mightst my seat forbear,
> And chide thy beauty and thy straying youth,
> Who lead thee in their riot even there
> Where thou art forc'd to break a two-fold truth—
>         Hers, by thy beauty tepting her to thee,
>         Thine, by thy beauty being false to me.

But here he makes it manifest that his forgiveness was full and complete:

No more be griev'd at that which thou hast done:
Roses have thorns, and silver fountains mud;
Clouds and eclipses stain both moon and sun,
And loathsome canker lives in sweetest bud.
All men make faults, and even I in this,
Authorising thy trespass with compare,
Myself corrupting, salving thy amiss,
Excusing thy sins more than thy sins are;
For to thy sensual fault I bring in sense—
The adverse party is thy advocate—
And 'gainst myself a lawful plea commence:
Such civil war is in my love and hate,
    That I an accessary needs must be
    To that sweet thief which sourly robs from me.

Shortly afterwards Shakespeare left London for Stratford (Sonnets 43–52), and when he returned Willie Hughes seems to have grown tired of the woman who for a little time had fascinated him. Her name is never mentioned again in the Sonnets, nor is there any allusion made to her. She had passed out of their lives.

But who was she? And, even if her name has not come down to us, were there any allusions to her in contemporary literature? It seems to me that although better educated than most of the women of her time, she was not nobly born, but was probably the profligate wife of some old and wealthy citizen. We know that women of this class, which was then first rising into social prominence, were strangely fascinated by the new art of stage-playing. They were to be found almost every afternoon at the theatre, when dramatic performances were being given, and *The Actors' Remonstrance* is eloquent on the subject of their amours with the young actors.

Cranley in his *Amanda* tells us of one who loved to mimic the actor's disguises, appearing one day "embroidered, laced, perfumed, in glittering show . . . as brave as any Countess," and the next day, "all in mourning, black and sad," now in the grey cloak of a country wench, and now "in the neat habit of a citizen." She was a curious woman, "more changeable and wavering than the moon," and the books that she loved to read were Shakespeare's *Venus and Adonis*, Beaumont's *Salmacis and Hermaphroditus*, amorous pamphlets, and "songs of love and sonnets exquisite." These sonnets that were to her the "books of her devotion," were surely none other but Shakespeare's own, for the whole description reads like the portrait of the woman who fell in love with Willie Hughes, and, lest we should have any doubt on the subject, Cranley, borrowing Shakespeare's play on words, tells us that, in her "proteus-like strange shapes," she is one who—

Changes hews with the chameleon.

Manningham's *Table-book*, also, contains a clear allusion to the same story. Manningham was a student at the Middle Temple with Sir Thomas Overbury and Edmund Curle, whose chambers he seems to have shared; and his *Diary* is still preserved among the Harleian MSS. at the British Museum, a small duodecimo book written in a fair and tolerably legible hand, and containing many unpublished anecdotes about Shakespeare, Sir Walter Raleigh, Spenser, Ben Jonson and others. The dates, which are inserted with much care, extend from January 1600-1 to April 1603, and under the heading "March 13, 1601," Manningham tells us that he heard from a member of Shakespeare's company that a certain citizen's wife being at the Globe Theatre one afternoon, fell in love with one of the actors, and "grew so farre in liking with him, that before shee went from the play shee appointed him to come that night unto hir," but that Shakespeare "overhearing their conclusion" anticipated his friend and came first to the lady's house, "went before and was entertained," as Manningham puts it, with some added looseness of speech which it is unnecessary to quote.

It seems to me that we had here a common and distorted version of the story that is revealed to us in the Sonnets, the story of the dark woman's love for Willie Hughes, and Shakespeare's mad attempt to make her love him in his friend's stead. It was not, of course, necessary to accept it as absolutely true in every detail. According to Manningham's informant, for instance, the name of the actor in question was not Willie Hughes, but Richard Burbage. Tavern gossip, however, is proverbially inaccurate, and Burbage was, no doubt, dragged into the story to give point to the foolish jest about William the Conqueror and Richard the Third, with which the entry in Manningham's *Diary* ends. Burbage was our first great tragic actor, but it needed all his genius to counterbalance the physical defects of low stature and corpulent figure under which he laboured, and he was not the sort of man who would have fascinated the dark woman of the Sonnets, or would have cared to be fascinated by her. There was no doubt that Willie Hughes was referred to, and the private diary of a young law student of the time thus curiously corroborated Cyril Graham's wonderful guess at the secret of Shakespeare's great romance. Indeed, when taken in conjunction with *Amanda*, Manningham's *Table-book* seemed to me to be an extremely strong link in the chain of evidence, and to place the new interpretation of the Sonnets on something like a secure historic basis, the fact that Cranley's poems was not published till after Shakespeare's death being really rather in favour of this view, as it was not likely that he would have ventured during the lifetime of the great dramatist to revive the memory of this tragic and bitter story.

This passion for the dark lady also enabled me to fix with still greater certainty the date of the Sonnets. From internal evidence, from the characteristics of language, style, and the like, it was evident that they belonged to Shakespeare's early period, the period of *Love's Labour's Lost* and *Venus and Adonis*. With the play, indeed, they are intimately connected. They display the same delicate euphuism, the same delight in fanciful phrase and curious expression, the artistic wilfulness and studied graces of the same "fair tongue, conceit's expositor," Rosaline, the

> whitely wanton with a velvet brow,
> With two pitch-balls stuck in her face for eyes,

who is born "to make black fair," and whose "favour turns the fashion of the days," is the dark lady of the Sonnets who makes black "beauty's successive heir." In the comedy as well as in the poems we have that half-sensuous philosophy that exalts the judgment of the senses "above all slower, more toilsome means of knowledge," and Berowne is perhaps, as Walter Pater suggests, a reflex of Shakespeare himself "when he has just become able to stand aside from and estimate the first period of his poetry."

Now though *Love's Labour's Lost* was not published till 1598, when it was brought out "newlie corrected and augmented" by Cuthbert Burby, there is no doubt that it was written and produced on the stage at a much earlier date, probably, as Professor Dowden points out, in 1588-9. If this be so, it is clear that Shakespeare's first meeting with Willie Hughes must have been in 1585, and it is just possible that this young actor may, after all, have been in his boyhood the musician of Lord Essex.

It is clear, at any rate, that Shakespeare's love for the dark lady must have passed away before 1594. In this year there appeared, under the editorship of Hadrian Dorell, that fascinating poem, or series of poems, *Willobie His Avisa*, which is described by Mr. Swinburne as the one contemporary book which has been supposed to throw any direct or indirect light on the mystic matter of the Sonnets. In it we learn how a young gentleman of St. John's College, Oxford, by name Henry Willobie, fell in love with a woman so "fair and chaste" that he called her Avisa, either because such beauty as hers had never been seen, or because she fled like a bird from the snare of his passion, and spread her wings for flight when he ventured but to touch her hand. Anxious to win his mistress, he consults his familiar friend W.S., "who not long before had tried the curtesy of the like passion, and was now newly recovered of the like infection." Shakespeare encouraged him in the siege that he is laying to the Castle of Beauty, telling him that every woman is to be wooed, and every woman to be won; views this "loving comedy" from far off, in order to see "whether it would sort to a happier end for this new actor than it did for the old player," and "enlargeth the wound with the sharpe razor of a willing conceit," feeling the purely æsthetic interest of the artist in the moods and emotions of others. It is unnecessary, however, to enter more fully into this curious passage in Shakespeare's life, as all that I wanted to point out was that in 1594 he had been cured of his infatuation for the dark lady, and had already been acquainted for at least three years with Willie Hughes.

My whole scheme of the Sonnets was now complete, and, by placing those that refer to the dark lady in their proper order and position, I saw the perfect unity and completeness of the whole. The drama—for indeed they formed a drama and a soul's tragedy of fiery passion and of noble thought—is divided into four scenes or acts. In the first of these (Sonnets 1–32) Shakespeare invites Willie Hughes to go upon the stage as an actor, and to put to the service of Art his wondeerful physical beauty, and his exquisite grace of youth, before passion has robbed him of the one, and time taken from him the other. Willie Hughes, after a time, consents to be a player in Shakespeare's company, and soon becomes the very centre and keynote of his inspiration. Suddenly, in one red-rose July (Sonnets 33–52, 61, and 127–152) there comes to the Globe Theatre a dark woman with wonderful eyes, who falls passionately in love with Willie Hughes. Shakespeare, sick with the malady of jealousy, and made mad by many doubts and fears, tries to fascinate the woman who had come between him and his friend. The love, that is at first feigned, becomes real, and he finds himself enthralled and dominated by a woman whom he knows to be evil and unworthy. To her the genius of a man is as nothing compared to a boy's beauty. Willie Hughes becomes for a time her slave and the toy of her fancy, and the second act ends with Shakespeare's departure from London. In the third act her influence has passed away. Shakespeare returns to London, and renews his friendship with Willie Hughes, to whom he promises immortality in his plays. Marlowe, hearing of the wonder and grace of the young actor, lures him away from the Globe Theatre to play Gaveston in the tragedy of *Edward II*, and for the second time Shakespeare is separated from his friend. The last act (Sonnets 100–126) tells us of the return of Willie Hughes to Shakespeare's company. Evil rumour has now stained the white purity of his name, but Shakespeare's love still endures and is perfect. Of the mystery of this love, and of the mystery of passion, we are told strange and marvellous things, and the Sonnets conclude with an envoi of twelve lines whose motive is the triumph of Beauty over Time, and of Death over Beauty.

And what had been the end of him who had been so dear to the soul of Shakespeare, and who by his presence and passion had given reality to Shakespeare's art? When the Civil War broke out, the English actors took the side of their king, and many of them, like Robinson foully slain by Major Harrison at the taking of Basing House, laid down their lives in the king's service. Perhaps on the trampled heath of Marston, or on the bleak hills of Naseby, the dead body of Willie Hughes had been found by some of the rough peasants of the district, his gold hair "dabbled with blood," and his breast pierced with many wounds. Or it may be that the Plague, which was very frequent in London at the beginning of the seventeenth century and was indeed regarded by many of the Christians as a judgment sent on the city for its love of "vaine plaies and idolatrous shewes," had touched the lad while he was acting, and he had crept home to his lodgings to die there alone, Shakespeare being far away at Stratford, and those who had flocked in such numbers to see him, the "gazers" whom, as the Sonnets tell us, he had "led astray," being too much afraid of contagion to come near him. A story of this kind was current at the time about a young actor, and was made use of by the Puritans in their attempts to stifle the free development of the English Renaissance. Yet, surely, had this actor been Willie Hughes, tidings of his tragic death would have been speedily brought to Shakespeare as he lay dreaming under the mulberry tree in his garden at New Place, and in an elegy as sweet as that written by Milton on Edward King, he would have mourned for the lad who had brought such joy and sorrow into his life, and whose connection with his art had been of so vital and intimate a character. Something made me feel certain that Willie Hughes had survived Shakespeare, and had fulfilled in some measure the high prophecies the poet had made about him, and one evening the true secret of his end flashed across me.

He had been one of those English actors who in 1611, the year of Shakespeare's retirement from the stage, went across sea to Germany and played before the great Duke Henry Julius of Brunswick, himself a dramatist of no mean order, and at the Court of that strange Elector of Brandenburg, who was so enamoured of beauty that he was said to have bought for his weight in amber the young son of a travelling Greek merchant, and to have given pageants in honour of his slave, all through that dreadful famine year of 1606-7, when the people died of hunger in the very streets of the town, and for the space of seven months there was no rain. The Library at Cassel contains to the present day a copy of the first edition of Marlowe's *Edward II*, the only copy in existence, Mr. Bullen tells us. Who could have brought it to that town but he who had created the part of the king's minion, and for whom indeed it had been written? Those stained and yellow pages had once been touched by his white hands. We also know that *Romeo and Juliet*, a play specially connected with Willie Hughes, was brought out at Dresden, in 1613, along with *Hamlet* and *King Lear*, and certain of Marlowe's plays, and it was surely to none other than Willie Hughes himself that in 1617 the death-mask of Shakespeare was brought by one of the suite of the English ambassador, pale token of the passing away of the great poet who had so dearly loved him. Indeed, there was something peculiarly fitting in the idea that the boy-actor, whose beauty had been so vital an element in the realism and romance of Shakespeare's art, had been the first to have brought to Germany the seed of the new culture, and was in his way the precursor of that *Aufklärung* or Illumination of the eighteenth century, that splendid movement which, though begun by Lessing and Herder, and brought to its full and perfect issue by Goethe was in no small part helped on by a young actor—Friedrich Schroeder—who awoke the popular consciousness, and by means of the feigned passions and mimetic methods of the stage showed the intimate, the vital, connection between life and literature. If this was so—and there was certainly no evidence against it—it was not improbable that Willie Hughes was one of those English comedians (*mimi quidam ex Britannia*, as the old chronicle calls them), who were slain at Nuremberg in a sudden uprising of the people, and were secretly buried in a little vineyard outside the city by some young men "who had found pleasure in their performances, and of whom some had sought to be instructed in the mysteries of the new art." Certainly no more fitting place could there be for him to whom Shakespeare had said "thou art all my art," than this little vineyard outside the city walls. For was it not from the sorrows of Dionysos that Tragedy sprang? Was not the light laughter of Comedy, with its careless merriment and quick replies, first heard on the lips of the Sicilian vine-dressers? Nay, did not the purple and red stain of the wine-froth on face and limbs give the first suggestion of the charm and fascination of disguise?—the desire for self-concealment, the sense of the value of objectivity, thus showing itself in the rude beginnings of the art. At any rate, wherever he lay—whether in the little vineyard at the gate of the Gothic town, or in some dim London churchyard amidst the roar and bustle of our great city—no gorgeous monument marked his resting place. His true tomb, as Shakespeare saw, was the poet's verse, his true monument the permanence of the drama. So had it been with others whose beauty had given a new creative impulse to their age. The ivory body of the Bithynian slave rots in the green ooze of the Nile, and on the yellow hills of the Cerameicus is strewn the dust of the young Athenian; but Antinous lives in sculpture, and Charmides in philosophy.

5

A young Elizabethan, who was enamoured of a girl so white that he named her Alba, has left on record the impression produced on him by one of the first performances of *Love's Labour's Lost*. Admirable though the actors were, and they played "in cunning wise," he tells us, especially those who took the lovers' parts, he was conscious that everything was "feigned," that nothing came "from the heart," that though they appeared to grieve they "felt no care," and were merely presenting "a show in jest." Yet, suddenly, this fanciful comedy of unreal romance became to him, as he sat in the audience, the real tragedy of his life. The moods of his own soul seemed to have taken shape and substance, and to be moving before him. His grief had a

mask that smiled, and his sorrow wore gay raiment. Behind the bright
and quickly-changing pageant of the stage, he saw himself, as one sees
one's image in a fantastic glass. The very words that came to the ac-
tors' lips were wrung out of his pain. Their false tears were of his
shedding.

There are few of us who have not felt something akin to this. We
become lovers when we see Romeo and Juliet, and Hamlet makes us
students. The blood of Duncan is upon our hands, with Timon we
rage against the world, and when Lear wanders out upon the heath
the terror of madness touches us. Ours is the white sinlessness of
Desdemona, and ours, also, the sin of Iago. Art, even the art of fullest
scope and widest vision, can never really show us the external world.
All that it shows us is our own soul, the one world of which we have
any real cognizance. And the soul itself, the soul of each one of us, is
to each one of us a mystery. It hides in the dark and broods, and
consciousness cannot tell us of its workings. Consciousness, indeed,
is quite inadequate to explain the contents of personality. It is Art,
and Art only, that reveals us to ourselves.

We sit at the play with the woman we love, or listen to the music in
some Oxford garden, or stroll with our friend through the cool galler-
ies of the Pope's house at Rome, and suddenly we become aware that
we have passions of which we have never dreamed, thoughts that make
us afraid, pleasures whose secret has been denied to us, sorrows that
have been hidden from our tears. The actor is unconscious of our
presence: the musician is thinking of the subtlety of the fugue, of the
tone of his instrument; the marble gods that smile so curiously at us
are made of insensate stone. But they have given form and substance
to what was within us; they have enabled us to realise our personality;
and a sense of perilous joy, or some touch or thrill of pain, or that
strange self-pity that man so often feels for himself, comes over us and
leaves us different.

Some such impression the Sonnets of Shakespeare had certainly
produced on me. As from opal dawns to sunsets of withered rose I
read and re-read them in garden or chamber, it seemed to me that I
was deciphering the story of a life that had once been mine, unrolling
the record of a romance that, without my knowing it, had coloured
the very texture of my nature, had dyed it with strange and subtle
dyes. Art, as so often happens, had taken the place of personal experi-
ence. I felt as if I had been initiated into the secret of that passionate
friendship, that love of beauty and beauty of love, of which Marsilio

Ficino tells us, and of which the Sonnets in their noblest and purest significance, may be held to be the perfect expression.

Yes: I had lived it all. I had stood in the round theatre with its open roof and fluttering banners, had seen the stage draped with black for a tragedy, or set with gay garlands for some brighter show. The young gallants came out with their pages, and took their seats in front of the tawny curtain that hung from the satyr-carved pillars of the inner scene. They were insolent and debonair in their fantastic dresses. Some of them wore French lovelocks, and white doublets stiff with Italian embroidery of gold thread, and long hose of blue or pale yellow silk. Others were all in black, and carried huge plumed hats. These affected the Spanish fashion. As they played at cards, and flew thin wreaths of smoke from the tiny pipes that the pages lit for them, the truant prentices and idle schoolboys that thronged the yard mocked them. But they only smiled at each other. In the side boxes some masked women were sitting. One of them was waiting with hungry eyes and bitten lips for the drawing back of the curtain. As the trumpet sounded for the third time she leant forward, and I saw her olive skin and raven's-wing hair. I knew her. She had marred for a season the great friendship of my life. Yet there was something about her that fascinated me.

The play changed according to my mood. Sometimes it was *Hamlet*. Taylor acted the Prince, and there were many who wept when Ophelia went mad. Sometimes it was *Romeo and Juliet*. Burbage was Romeo. He hardly looked the part of the young Italian, but there was a rich music in his voice, and passionate beauty in every gesture. I saw *As You Like It*, and *Cymbeline*, and *Twelfth Night*, and in each play there was some one whose life was bound up into mine, who realised for me every dream, and gave shape to every fancy. How gracefully he moved! The eyes of the audience were fixed on him.

And yet it was in this century that it had all happened. I had never seen my friend, but he had been with me for many years, and it was to his influence that I owed my passion for Greek thought and art, and indeed all my sympathy with the Hellenic spirit. (Φιλοσοφεῖν μὲτ᾽ ἐρωτος!) How that phrase had stirred me in my Oxford days! I did not understand then why it was so. But I knew now. There had been a presence beside me always. Its silver feet had trod night's shadowy meadows, and the white hands had moved aside the trembling curtains of the dawn. It had walked with me through the grey cloisters, and when I sat reading I my room, it was there also. What though I had been unconscious of it? The soul had a life of its own, and the brain its own sphere of action. There was something within us that knew nothing of sequence or extension, and yet, like the philosopher of the Ideal City, was the spectator of all time and of all existence. It had senses that quickened, passions that came to birth, spiritual ecstasies of contemplation, ardours of fiery-coloured love. It was we who were unreal, and our conscious life was the least important part of our development. The soul, the secret soul, was the only reality.

How curiously it had all been revealed to me! A book of Sonnets, published nearly three hundred years ago, written by a dead hand and in honour of a dead youth, had suddenly explained to me the whole story of my soul's romance. I remembered how once in Egypt I had been present at the opening of a frescoed coffin that had been found in one of the basalt tombs at Thebes. Inside there was the body of a young girl swathed in tight bands of linen, and with a gilt mask over her face. As I stooped down to look at it, I had seen that one of the little withered hands held a scroll of yellow papyrus covered with strange characters. How I wished now that I had had it read to me! It might have told me something more about the soul that hid within me, and had its mysteries of passion of which I was kept in ignorance. Strange, that we knew so little about ourselves, and that our most intimate personality was concealed from us! Were we to look in tombs for our real life, and in art for the legend of our days?

Week after week, I pored over these poems, and each new form of knowledge seemed to me a mode of reminiscence. Finally, after two months had elapsed, I determined to make a strong appeal to Erskine to do justice to the memory of Cyril Graham, and to give to the world his marvellous interpretation of the Sonnets—the only interpretation that thoroughly explained the problem. I have not any copy of my letter, I regret to say, nor have I been able to lay my hand upon the original; but I remember that I went over the whole ground, and covered sheets of paper with passionate reiteration of the arguments and proofs that my study had suggested to me.

It seemed to me that I was not merely restoring Cyril Graham to his proper place in literary history, but rescuing the honour of Shakespeare himself front the tedious memory of a commonplace intrigue. I put into the letter all my enthusiasm. I put into the letter all my faith.

No sooner, in fact, had I sent it off than a curious reaction came over me. It seemed to me that I had given away my capacity for belief in the Willie Hughes theory of the Sonnets, that something had gone out of me, as it were, and that I was perfectly indifferent to the whole subject. What was it that had happened? It is difficult to say. Perhaps, by finding perfect expression for a passion, I had exhausted the passion itself. Emotional forces, like the forces of physical life, have their positive limitations. Perhaps the mere effort to convert any one to a theory involves some form of renunciation of the power of credence. Influence is simply a transference of personality, a mode of giving away what is most precious to one's self, and its exercise produces a sense, and, it may be, a reality of loss. Every disciple takes away something from his master. Or perhaps I had become tired of the whole thing, wearied of its fascination, and, my enthusiasm having burnt out, my reason was left to its own unimpassioned judgment. However it came about, and I cannot pretend to explain it, there was no doubt that Willie Hughes suddenly became to me a mere myth, an idle dream, the boyish fancy of a young man who, like most ardent spirits, was more anxious to convince others than to be himself convinced.

I must admit that this was a bitter disappointment to me. I had gone through every phase of this great romance. I had lived with it, and it had become part of my nature. How was it that it had left me? Had I touched upon some secret that my soul desired to conceal? Or was there no permanence in personality? Did things come and go through the brain, silently, swiftly, and without footprints, like shadows through a mirror? Were we at the mercy of such impressions as Art or Life chose to give us? It seemed to me to be so.

It was at night-time that this feeling first came to me. I had sent my servant out to post the letter to Erskine, and was seated at the window looking out at the blue and gold city. The moon had not yet risen, and there was only one star in the sky, but the streets were full of quick-moving and flashing lights, and the windows of Devonshire House were illuminated for a great dinner to be given to some of the foreign princes then visiting London. I saw the scarlet liveries of the royal carriages, and the crowd hustling about the sombre gates of the court-yard.

Suddenly, I said to myself: "I have been dreaming, and all my life for these two months has been unreal. There was no such person as Willie Hughes." Something like a faint cry of pain came to my lips as I began to realise how I had deceived myself, and I buried my face in my hands, struck with a sorrow greater than any I had felt since boyhood. After a few moments I rose, and going into the library took up the Sonnets, and began to read them. But it was all to no avail. They gave me back nothing of the feeling that I had brought to them; they revealed to me nothing of what I had found hidden in their lines. Had I merely been influenced by the beauty of the forged portrait, charmed by that Shelley-like face into faith and credence? Or, as Erskine had suggested, was it the pathetic tragedy of Cyril Graham's death that had so deeply stirred me? I could not tell. To the present day I cannot understand the beginning or the end of this strange passage in my life.

However, as I had said some very unjust and bitter things to Erskine in my letter, I determined to go and see him as soon as possible, and to make my apologies to him for my behaviour. Accordingly, the next morning I drove down to Birdcage Walk, where I found him sitting in his library, with the forged picture of Willie Hughes in front of him.

"My dear Erskine!" I cried, "I have come to apologise to you."

"To apologise to me?" he said. "What for?"

"For my letter," I answered.

"You have nothing to regret in your letter," he said. "On the contrary, you have done me the greatest service in your power. You have shown me that Cyril Graham's theory is perfectly sound."

I stared at him in blank wonder.

"You don't mean to say that you believe in Willie Hughes?" I exclaimed.

"Why not?" he rejoined. "You have proved the thing to me. Do you think I cannot estimate the value of evidence?"

"But there is no evidence at all," I groaned, sinking into a chair. "When I wrote to you I was under the influence of a perfectly silly enthusiasm. I had been touched by the story of Cyril Graham's death, fascinated by his artistic theory, enthralled by the wonder and novelty of the whole idea. I see now that the theory is based on a delusion. The only evidence for the existence of Willie Hughes is that picture in front of you, and that picture is a forgery. Don't be carried away by mere sentiment in this matter. Whatever romance may have to say about the Willie Hughes theory, reason is dead against it."

"I don't understand you," said Erskine, looking at me in amazement. "You have convinced me by your letter that Willie Hughes is an absolute reality. Why have you changed your mind? Or is all that you have been saying to me merely a joke?"

"I cannot explain it to you," I rejoined, "but I see now that there is really nothing to be said in favour of Cyril Graham's interpretation. The Sonnets may not be addressed to Lord Pembroke. They probably are not. But for heaven's sake don't waste your time in a foolish attempt to discover a young Elizabethan actor who never existed, and to make a phantom puppet the centre of the great cycle of Shakespeare's Sonnets."

"I see that you don't understand the theory," he replied.

"My dear Erskine," I cried, "not understand it! Why, I feel as if I had invented it. Surely my letter shows you that I not merely went into the whole matter, but that I contributed proofs of every kind. The one flaw in the theory is that it presupposes the existence of the person whose existence is the subject of dispute. If we grant that there was in Shakespeare's company a young actor of the name of Willie Hughes, it is not difficult to make him the object of the Sonnets. But as we know that there was no actor of this name in the company of the Globe Theatre, it is idle to pursue the investigation further."

"But that is exactly what we don't know," said Erskine. "It is quite true that his name does not occur in the list given in the first folio; but, as Cyril pointed out, that is rather a proof in favour of the existence of Willie Hughes than against it, if we remember his treacherous desertion of Shakespeare for a rival dramatist. Besides," and here I must admit that Erskine made what seems to me now a rather good point, though, at the time, I laughed at it, "there is no reason at all why Willie Hughes should not have gone upon the stage under an assumed name. In fact it is extremely probably that he did so. We know that there was a very strong prejudice against the theatre in his day, and nothing is more likely than that his family insisted upon his adopting some *nom de plume*. The editors of the first folio would naturally put him down under his stage name, the name by which he was best known to the public, but the Sonnets were of course an entirely different matter, and in the dedication to them the publisher very properly addresses him under his real initials. If this be so, and it seems to me the most simple and rational explanation of the matter, I regard Cyril Graham's theory as absolutely proved."

"But what evidence have you?" I exclaimed, laying my hand on his. "You have no evidence at all. It is mere hypothesis. And which of Shakespeare's actors do you think that Willie Hughes was? The 'pretty fellow' Ben Jonson tells us of, who was so fond of dressing up in girls' clothes?"

"I don't know," he answered rather irritably. "I have not had time to investigate the point yet. But I feel quite sure that my theory is the true one. Of course it is a hypothesis, but then it is a hypothesis that explains everything, and if you had been sent to Cambridge to study science, instead of to Oxford to dawdle over literature, you would know that a hypothesis that explains everything is a certainty."

"Yes, I am aware that Cambridge is a sort of educational institute," I murmured. "I am glad I was not there."

"My dear fellow," said Erskine, suddenly turning his keen grey eyes on me, "you believe in Cyril Graham's theory, you believe in Willie Hughes, you know that the Sonnets are addressed to an actor, but for some reason or other you won't acknowledge it."

"I wish I could believe it," I rejoined. "I would give anything to be able to do so. But I can't. It is a sort of moonbeam theory, very lovely, very fascinating, but intangible. When one thinks that one has got hold of it, it escapes one. No: Shakespeare's heart is still to us 'a closet never pierc'd with crystal eyes,' as he calls it in one of the sonnets. We shall never know the true secret of the passion of his life."

Erskine sprang from the sofa, and paced up and down the room. "We know it already," he cried, "and the world shall know it some day."

I had never seen him so excited. He would not hear of my leaving him, and insisted on my stopping for the rest of the day.

We argued the matter over for hours, but nothing that I could say could make him surrender his faith in Cyril Graham's interpretation. He told me that he intended to devote his life to proving the theory, and that he was determined to do justice to Cyril Graham's memory. I entreated him, laughed at him, begged of him, but it was of no use. Finally we parted, not exactly in anger, but certainly with a shadow between us. He thought me shallow, I thought him foolish. When I called on him again, his servant told me that he had gone to Germany. The letters I wrote to him remained unanswered.

Two years afterwards, as I was going into my club, the hall porter handed me a letter with a foreign postmark. It was from Erskine, and written at the Hôtel d'Angleterre, Cannes. When I had read it, I was filled with horror, though I did not quite believe that he would be so mad as to carry his resolve into execution. The gist of the letter was that he had tried in every way to verify the Willie Hughes theory, and had failed, and that as Cyril Graham had given his life for this theory, he himself had determined to give his own life also to the same cause. The concluding words of the letter were these: "I still believe in Willie

Hughes; and by the time you receive this, I shall have died by my own hand for Willie Hughes' sake: for his sake, and for the sake of Cyril Graham, whom I drove to his death by my shallow scepticism and ignorant lack of faith. The truth was once revealed to you, and you rejected it. It comes to you now, stained with the blood of two lives—do not turn away from it."

It was a horrible moment. I felt sick with misery, and yet I could not believe that he would carry out his intention. To die for one's theological opinions is the worst use a man can make of his life; but to die for a literary theory! It seemed impossible.

I looked at the date. The letter was a week old. Some unfortunate chance had prevented my going to the club for several days, or I might have got it in time to save him. Perhaps it was not too late. I drove off to my rooms, packed up my things, and started by the night mail from Charing Cross. The journey was intolerable. I thought I would never arrive.

As soon as I did, I drove to the Hôtel d'Angleterre. It was quite true. Erskine was dead. They told me that he had been buried two days before in the English cemetery. There was something horribly grotesque about the whole tragedy. I said all kinds of wild things, and the people in the hall looked curiously at me.

Suddenly Lady Erskine, in deep mourning, passed across the vestibule. When she saw me she came up to me, murmured something about her poor son, and burst into tears. I led her into her sitting room. An elderly gentleman was there, reading a newspaper. It was the English doctor.

We talked a great deal about Erskine, but I said nothing about his motive for committing suicide. It was evident that he had not told his mother anything about the reason that had driven him to so fatal, so mad an act. Finally Lady Erskine rose and said, "George left you something as a memento. It was a thing he prized very much. I will get it for you."

As soon as she had left the room I turned to the doctor and said, "What a dreadful shock it must have been for Lady Erskine! I wonder that she bears it as well as she does."

"Oh, she knew for months past that it was coming," he answered.

"Knew it for months past!" I cried. "But why didn't she stop him? Why didn't she have him watched? He must have been out of his mind."

The doctor stared at me. "I don't know what you mean," he said.

"Well," I cried, "if a mother knows that her son is going to commit suicide—"

"Suicide!" he answered. "Poor Erskine did not commit suicide. He died of consumption. He came here to die. The moment I saw him I knew that there was no chance. One lung was almost gone, and the other was very much affected. Three days before he died he asked me was there any hope. I told him frankly that there was none, and that he had only a few days to live. He wrote some letters, and was quite resigned, retaining his senses to the last."

I got up from my seat, and going over to the open window I looked out on the crowded promenade. I remember that the brightly-coloured umbrellas and gay parasols seemed to me like huge fantastic butter-flies fluttering by the shore of a blue-metal sea, and that the heavy odour of violets that came across the garden made me think of that wonderful sonnet in which Shakespeare tells us that the scent of these flowers always reminded him of his friend. What did it all mean? Why had Erskine written me that extraordinary letter? Why when standing at the very gate of death had he turned back to tell me what was not true? Was Hugo right? Is affectation the only thing that accompanies a man up the steps of the scaffold? Did Erskine merely want to pro-duce a dramatic effect? That was not like him. It was more like some-thing I might have done myself. No: he was simply actuated by a desire to reconvert me to Cyril Graham's theory, and he thought that if I could be made to believe that he too had given his life for it, I would be deceived by the pathetic fallacy of martyrdom. Poor Erskine! I had grown wiser since I had seen him. Martyrdom was to me merely a tragic form of scepticism, an attempt to realise by fire what one had failed to do by faith. No man dies for what he knows to be true. Men die for what they want to be true, for what some terror in their hearts tells them is not true. The very uselessness of Erskine's letter made me doubly sorry for him. I watched the people strolling in and out of the cafés, and wondered if any of them had known him. The white dust blew down the scorched sunlit road, and the feathery palms moved restlessly in the shaken air.

At that moment Lady Erskine returned to the room carrying the fatal picture of Willie Hughes. "When George was dying, he begged me to give you this," she said. As I took it from her, her tears fell on my hand.

This curious work of art hangs now in my library, where it is very much admired by my artistic friends, one of whom has etched it for me. They have decided that it is not a Clouet, but an Ouvry. I have never cared to tell them its true history, but sometimes, when I look at it, I think there is really a great deal to be said for the Willie Hughes theory of Shakespeare's Sonnets.

# AMERICAN LITERATURE

*Little Women* — Louisa May Alcott
*The Last of the Mohicans* — James Fenimore Cooper
*The Red Badge of Courage* and *Maggie* — Stephen Crane
*Selected Poems* — Emily Dickinson
*Narrative of the Life and Other Writings* — Frederick Douglass
*The Scarlet Letter* — Nathaniel Hawthorne
*The Call of the Wild* and *White Fang* – Jack London
*Moby-Dick* — Herman Melville
*Major Tales and Poems* — Edgar Allan Poe
*The Jungle* — Upton Sinclair
*Uncle Tom's Cabin* — Harriet Beecher Stowe
*Walden* and *Civil Disobedience* — Henry David Thoreau
*Adventures of Huckleberry Finn* — Mark Twain
*The Complete Adventures of Tom Sawyer* — Mark Twain
*Ethan Frome* and *Summer* — Edith Wharton
*Leaves of Grass* — Walt Whitman


# WORLD LITERATURE

*The Divine Comedy* — Dante Alighieri
*Tales from the 1001 Nights* — Sir Richard Burton
*Don Quixote* — Miguel de Cervantes
*Crime and Punishment* — Fyodor Dostoevsky
*The Count of Monte Cristo* — Alexandre Dumas
*The Three Musketeers* — Alexandre Dumas
*The Iliad* — Homer
*The Odyssey* — Homer
*The Hunchback of Notre-Dame* — Victor Hugo
*Les Misérables* — Victor Hugo
*The Phantom of the Opera* — Gaston Leroux
*The Prince* — Niccolò Machiavelli

# BRITISH LITERATURE

*Emma* — Jane Austen
*Pride and Prejudice* — Jane Austen
*Sense and Sensibility* — Jane Austen
*Peter Pan* — J. M. Barrie
*Jane Eyre* — Charlotte Brontë
*Wuthering Heights* — Emily Brontë
*Alice in Wonderland* — Lewis Carroll
*Robinson Crusoe* — Daniel Defoe
*A Christmas Carol and Other Holiday Tales* — Charles Dickens
*Great Expectations* — Charles Dickens
*A Tale of Two Cities* — Charles Dickens
*A Passage to India* — E. M. Forster
*The Sonnets and Other Love Poems* — William Shakespeare
*Three Romantic Tragedies* — William Shakespeare
*Frankenstein* — Mary Shelley
*Dr. Jekyll and Mr. Hyde and Other Strange Tales* — Robert Louis Stevenson
*Treasure Island* — Robert Louis Stevenson
*Dracula* — Bram Stoker
*Gulliver's Travels* — Jonathan Swift
*The Time Machine* and *The War of the Worlds* — H. G. Wells
*The Picture of Dorian Gray* — Oscar Wilde

# ANTHOLOGIES

*Four Centuries of Great Love Poems*

**BORDERS.**
**CLASSICS**

The text of this book is set in 11 point Goudy Old Style, designed by American printer and typographer Frederic W. Goudy (1865–1947).

The archival-quality, natural paper is composed of recyclable products made from wood grown in sustainable forests; the manufacturing processes conform to the environmental regulations of the country of origin.

The finished volume demonstrates the convergence of Old-World craftsmanship and modern technology that exemplifies books manufactured by Edwards Brothers, Inc. Established in 1893, the family-owned business is a well-respected leader in book manufacturing, recognized the world over for quality and attention to detail.

In addition, Ann Arbor Media Group's editorial and design services provide full-service book publication to business partners.